THE GOD
OF HOLY FIRE

BY

TIMOTHY D. JOHNSON

DEDICATION

I dedicate this book to my dear, sweet mother, Joan Weddle. Her continual love, nurturing and encouragement throughout my life, gave me the strength to push beyond my limits. Thank you, Mother, for the years sacrifice and devotion! I pray this book greatly blesses you, and all who read it!

FOREWORD

This book was written by *revelation*. During my daily prayer time, the Lord began to stir me towards the writing of this book. He asked me to set aside everything else I was doing at the time, so I could *focus* on what He wanted to bring forth. He caused me to understand the importance of His request.

The Lord made it clear to me that <u>He</u> wanted to write this book *through* me. He sent His Spirit into my heart with specific directives. One of those instructions, as I wrote each day, was to ask the Lord for Divine unction, and to lift up prayer, asking Jesus to disclose the *exact* things that He desired to reveal about Himself in this work. To the best of my ability, I honored that request daily.

I felt the fire of His Presence as I wrote! Although much of the content of this book might already be *knowledge* to many; it was a *revelation* to me.

That which the Lord spoke to me, I wrote. I quickly learned during the writing of this book that our God *still* speaks from the Fire!

Through this book, I have also learned much about the ways of God and His character. I experienced a much deeper understanding of His Truth, Holiness, and of the longings of the heart of God through the Fire of His Jealousy!

Most importantly, I now understand how the Fire of God can transform man when it engulfs the human heart.

Timothy Johnson

THE KINGS TABLE

CHAPTER ONE
A NAMELESS GOD

Chapter One
A Nameless God

The authorship for writing the Book of Genesis, which means "the beginning," is traditionally credited to Moses. In that book, God is referred to by several different names, each coming from different perspectives of how man *experienced* God at a specific moment in time.

The first name attributed to God in the Bible was *Elohim*, meaning "strength" or "power." It often bore the unusual characteristic of being used in plural form (although not always the case). In Genesis 1:1 we read "In the beginning, *Elohim* created the heaven and the earth."

Elohim was the name used to refer to God about 2,300 times throughout the Bible, often with added compound words to detail specific characteristics or attributes of God like these:

- *Elohim Kedem* - God of the Beginning (Deut. 33:27)
- *Elohim Mishpat* - God of Justice (Isaiah 30:18)
- *Elohim Selichot* - God of Forgiveness (Nehemiah 9:17)
- *Elohim Marom* - God of Heights (Micah 6:6)
- *Elohim Mikarov* - God Who Is Near (Jeremiah 23:23)
- *Elohim Mauzi* - God of My Strength (Psalm 43:2)
- *Elohim Tehilati* - God of My Praise (Psalm 109:1)
- *Elohim Yishi* - God of My Salvation (Psalm 18:46)
- *Elohim Kedoshim* - Holy God (Leviticus 19:2)
- *Elohim Chaiyim* - Living God (Jer. 10:10, Deut. 10:17)

From the very beginning, these names were simply man appointed titles for God, but not the actual name that this living God would eventually reveal to man about Himself.

The Bible contains interesting encounters where people have heard the "audible" voice of God before, but far more often you will see down through the Scriptures, that interactions with the Lord frequently resulted in a manifestation of God - with the appearance of Holy Fire! Did you say fire? Really? Fire? Yes, down through Bible history, the Holy Fire of God became not only His signature but even His very seal!

In Genesis 15 we can begin to see this visible manifestation of God as He revealed Himself through fire! This encounter became one of the most important meetings ever between God and man! It happened on Mt. Hermon, the place where God cut a covenant with Abram, (also the same place where thousands of years later the transfiguration of Christ occurred).

The Lord tells Abram He is going to become his shield and his exceedingly great reward. But Abram says, "how can this be for I am childless with no heir of my own?" At that point, the Lord made an astonishing promise to Abram, saying that an heir would indeed come forth – from Abram's own body! Abram believed God – and to him, it was accounted to Abram for righteousness.

Then the Lord had Abram go outside and showed him the stars. The Lord promised Abram that He would make his offspring as numerous as the stars! The Lord promised to give Abram much land – both to him and his descendants, but Abram asked the Lord for *confirmation* that he would indeed inherit such land.

Instead of just assuring Abram that He would do it, the Lord did an unusual thing… He told Abram to bring Him a heifer, goat, ram, turtledove, and pigeon. Abram then cut some of the animals in half, placing them opposite from each other, and then God caused Abram to fall into a deep sleep.

The Bible tells us that darkness and terror fell upon Abram as he slept, and the Lord spoke to Abram prophetically, telling him that his descendants would eventually become slaves for 400 years, but that the Lord would bring them up out of slavery, along with many great possessions.

Then the most amazing thing happened! While the Lord was speaking to Abram in this dream-like state, an oven suddenly appeared before Abram, filled with smoke and with burning fire! It was a *manifestation* of God's fiery Presence, and this same Holy Fire then passed between the animals! The Hebrew language describes this fire of His Presence as a "burning lamp" or a "fiery torch."

As God made this oath to Abram that his descendants would possess the land, the Lord *consummated* His covenant with man, by passing through the sacrifice with the fire of His Presence to seal His Holy Covenant! God seals Covenant in Holy Fire!

Sodom and Gomorrah are two cities on the Jordan River plain, around the area of the Dead Sea. The sin and wickedness in these cities had become so vile the Bible tells us:

> And the LORD said, "Because the outcry against Sodom
> and Gomorrah is great, and because their sin is very grave, I
> (singular) *will go down now and see whether they have done*

13

altogether according to the outcry against it that has come to
Me; and if not, I will know." (Genesis 18:20-21)

The Lord had determined not to hide from Abram (now called Abraham) what He was about to do with both Sodom and Gomorrah. As Abraham stood before God, the Lord said:

"Shall I hide from Abraham what I am doing, since Abraham
shall surely become a great and mighty nation and all the nations
of the earth shall be blessed in him?" (Genesis 18:17-18)

Once Abraham understood what the Lord intended to do, the Bible gives us the first real look at the role of a true intercessor, standing in the gap and pleading before God. Abraham said:

"Would You also destroy the righteous with the wicked?
Suppose there were fifty righteous within the city; would You
also, destroy the place and not spare it for the fifty righteous that
were in it? Far be it from You to do such a thing as this, to slay
the righteous with the wicked, so that the righteous should be
As the wicked; far be it from You! Shall not the Judge of all the
earth do right?" (Genesis 18:23-25)

As a result of his intercession, Abraham ended up turning the heart of the God, and the Lord agreed to spare Sodom if fifty righteous people could be found in that city.

But Abraham continued to entreat the Lord, asking Him if He would do the same if only forty-five righteous people could be found in that city. This negotiation continued until Abraham successfully pleaded with God down to an agreement that if there were at least ten righteous people found in Sodom, the Lord would spare the city.

Unfortunately, there were not even ten righteous people found in the entire city! Angels then came and helped remove Lot and

14

his family from the city. During their rescue, they were warned not to look back at the city that was about to be destroyed, but Lot's wife disobeyed the warning, and as she looked back, she instantly turned into a pillar of salt!

In what could be called *"the terror of the Lord,"* the Bible says:

> *"Then the LORD rained brimstone and **fire** on Sodom and Gomorrah, **from the LORD out of Heaven**. So He overthrew those cities, all the plain, all the inhabitants of the cities, and what grew on the ground." (Genesis 19:24-25)*

The purifying power of the Holy Fire of God came that day in judgment, raining down from heaven, and cleansed the land. We will learn as we read this book, the fire of God can come either in *blessing*, or it can come in *judgment*. This fire wasn't just any *"fire,"* this fire came from the Most High God! At this stage of Bible history, man was only just beginning to learn about the Holy Fire of God!

From Adam to Moses there was a span of 26 generations. All during those years this loving and faithful, yet ever mysterious God, had remained *nameless* - all the way until we reach Mt. Sinai in the third chapter of Exodus!

It's important to remember the context here. Moses was widely believed to be not only the author of Genesis but also the entire Pentateuch or first five books of the Bible; Genesis, Exodus, Leviticus, Numbers, and Deuteronomy (except for the last eight verses of Deuteronomy, which were written, and inserted by Joshua about the death of Moses).

As Moses wrote, he constantly referred to the name of God as *Elohim*, but there were also many instances in those five books where Moses penned the "true" name of God... *Jehovah* (or YHWH) all the way back to *Genesis 2:4*, even though it wasn't until *Exodus 3:4* that God revealed His true name to man.

How can this be? Each time Moses referred to God's true name, remember, it was as he was recounting the history of Israel <u>from a later date</u>. He was inserting God's true name from a "present tense" posture (as he wrote), because at the time of his writings, Moses had already *learned* the true name of God.

But now, let's get back to this *nameless* God in Chapter 3 of Exodus... the Lord was about to reveal more about Himself to man in that encounter - than he had ever known about God! This revelation happened on Mt. Sinai (also called Mt. Horeb), which eventually became known as the mountain of fire!

The phenomenal experience that Moses had that day with God upon Mt. Sinai stands out as one of the most significant events throughout the entire course of biblical history!

At the outset of Exodus, Chapter 3, Moses was tending his flocks, when he encountered an unusual *manifestation* of God – in a burning bush!

For God chose to reveal His Manifest Presence to man within this burning bush - as Holy Fire (God called even the ground around that very place, Holy). It was from the midst of this Holy Fire that God revealed His Most Holy name to Moses. The Lord declared to Moses "**I AM** who **I AM.**"

But exactly who was this "**I AM**" speaking from the fire? Was it the entire Godhead? Was it the Father? Was it the Son? Was it the Holy Spirit? Could it have just been an Angel sent forth to speak *for* God since He was called *"The Angel of the Lord?"*

Good question! For even a modest study of the Bible details many possible *appearances* of God to man throughout the Old Testament. These appearances of God are called *Theophanies* (which are manifestations of God's Presence upon the earth during the Old Testament period). But a closer examination of Scriptures concerning these manifestations reveal an even more startling fact… some of these appearances of God were from a distinct, (singular) *person* of the Godhead!

Understanding exactly which *person* of the Godhead was being revealed through these manifestations is paramount to our study on the Holy Fire of God because we will see that this *person* of the Godhead will continue to reveal Himself to man down through the rest of the entire Bible! And that His appearance almost always came in the form of a manifestation of Holy Fire! Are you serious?

Let's take a closer look *into* the Word of God. The *Logos.*

> *"And the **Angel of the LORD** appeared to Moses **in a flame of fire**
> From the midst of a bush. So he looked, and behold, the bush was
> burning with fire, but the bush was not consumed." (Exodus 3:2)*

You will (surprisingly) discover that well-meaning, and respected Bible scholars remain deeply divided about just who this *"Angel of the LORD"* was… Some questioned whether this manifestation in the burning bush was truly God Himself, while others questioned whether this was a true *Theophany*, a *Christophany* or even an *Angelophany*?

I believe we can answer this, but let's first try to break down what these words mean so we can have a clearer understanding of exactly what these scholars are referencing.

The Easton's Bible Dictionary defines these words as:

Theophany. A temporarily visible manifestation of the Presence and Glory of God. This may occur in natural phenomena such as cloud or fire, in human form, or prophetic visionary experience.

Christophany. A Christophany is a physical appearance of Jesus Christ in the Old Testament. Since the Old Testament (Genesis-Malachi) was written before the "incarnation" of Christ, therefore every Christophany is an appearance of the "pre-incarnate" Messiah, Jesus Christ.

Angelophany. The visible manifestation of an angel or angels sent by God unto man.

Scholars from the *Angelophany* camp argue that the burning bush was just an ***Angel of the Lord*** appearing to Moses, just *representing* God because the Hebrew word for "Angel" means a "Messenger" or one sent *from* God. They argue that the Scripture says it was *"An Angel of the Lord appeared unto Moses."*

True, the Scriptures do say *"An Angel of the Lord..."* but the author of this book would argue that position is not well supported since this *"Angel of the Lord"* spoke in a "first person" tense (vernacular).

> *"So when the **LORD** saw that he turned aside to look,*
> ***God*** *called to him from the midst of the bush*
> *and said, "Moses, Moses!" And he said, "Here I am."*

*Then He said, "Do not draw near this place. Take your sandals off your feet, for the place where you stand, is Holy Ground." Moreover, He said, <u>'I, (first person) **am the God of your father — the God of Abraham, the God of Isaac, and the God of Jacob.'**</u> And Moses hid his face, for he was afraid to look upon <u>**God**</u>." (Exodus 3:4-6)*

A closer study of the entire 3rd chapter of Exodus reveals that God referred to Himself, using the word "**I**" or "**I AM**" some fourteen times. Each time "**I**" was used – it was a "first person" tense, meaning the direct reference or inference from the *actual* person identified as speaking! (i.e. "*<u>I am the God</u> of Abraham, Isaac, and Jacob"*), with no indication as one speaking on behalf of another!

We believe that the Lord God of Heaven is three distinct *persons* in One – the Trinity of God. But the Lord spoke in a singular tense that day upon Mt. Sinai, representing one distinct *person* of the Trinity, for He spoke in a "first person" tense (singular).

So, which *person* of the Godhead was manifested in the burning bush? Can we rule out it as being the *person* of the Father that Moses **saw** on Mt. Sinai since Scripture quotes Jesus as saying:

*"<u>**No one**</u> has <u>**seen**</u> the Father, except He who is from God; He has seen the Father." (John 6:46)*

Could it have been the Holy Spirt of God present that day in the burning bush? Certainly, we can see the specific role and *person* of the Holy Spirit at work in the earth from creation as He brooded over the waters and beyond. We continue to see the work of the Holy Spirit as He endowed men and women in strength, artistry, and revelations in the Old Testament. And then, of course, His incredible work in the New Testament, empowering the Church at Pentecost and beyond, so could it have been the distinct *person* of the Holy Spirit as the one who was speaking from the burning bush that day?

What about a *Christophany*? Could the manifestation of fire in the burning bush that day have been the distinct revelation of Jesus Christ, according to His role and service in the Trinity?

Scholars from the *Theophany* camp say these manifestations represent a *general* Presence of God, as they identify and acknowledge Deity, but they fall well short of attributing this manifestation to a distinct (singular) *person* of the Godhead.

Recognizing *Theophanies* in the Bible are important for coming into a deeper understanding of both the intentionality (purposes) of God and His characteristics, yet from a classic standpoint, the basic understanding of a *Theophany* is like looking into the depths of God with only a 10X (power) microscope. But an average microscope kit comes with three lenses; 10X, 40X and 400X! It takes a minimum 400X lens to study cells and cell structure. Wouldn't you rather put on the more powerful 400X lens so you can see deeper into the *Logos*?

The author believes through the reliability of Scripture, that a preponderance of further evidence exists that the fiery *Presence* revealed in the burning bush that day was not only God Himself, but to be even more specific – that it was Christ, revealing His true nature, intentions, and even His name!

But to fully answer this, let's first put to rest once and for all - the core question itself, namely, was it truly God Himself (Deity) that was manifested to Moses at Mt. Sinai and not just an Angel sent *from* God?

When you place a 400X power magnifying lens on, we can look even more *closely* (while relying completely on) the Word of God. In <u>numerous</u> places, the Bible unequivocally declares that it was truly **<u>God</u>** Himself speaking from the burning bush! Just look at all these supporting Scriptures in the Bible:

"With the precious things of the earth and its fullness,
*And the favor of **<u>Him</u>** <u>who dwelt in the bush</u>.*
Let the blessing come 'on the head of Joseph,
And on the crown of the head of him who was
separate from his brothers." (Deuteronomy 33:16)

"But concerning the dead, that they rise, have you not read in
*the book of Moses<u>, in the burning bush passage</u>, how **<u>God</u>** spoke*
*to him, saying, '**<u>I am the God</u>** of Abraham, the God of Isaac,*
and the God of Jacob'?" (Mark 12:26)

"But even Moses showed <u>in the burning bush passage</u>
*that the dead are raised, when he called **<u>the Lord</u>** 'the God*
of Abraham, the God of Isaac, and the God of Jacob." (Luke 20:37)

"And when forty years had passed, an Angel of the Lord
appeared to him <u>in a flame of fire in a bush</u>, in the wilderness
of Mount Sinai. When Moses saw it, he marveled at the sight;
*and as he drew near to observe, **<u>the voice of the Lord</u>** came to*
*him, saying, '**<u>I am the God</u>** <u>of your fathers — the God of Abraham,</u>*
<u>the God of Isaac, and the God of Jacob</u>. 'And Moses trembled and
*dared not look. 'Then **<u>the LORD</u>** said to him, "Take your sandals off*
your feet, for the place where you stand, is holy ground." (Acts 7:30-33)

Now wouldn't you think it safe, through the abundance of Scriptures stated here, that the fiery *Presence* at the burning bush was indeed God Himself? Splendid!

But now back to the burning question (pardon the pun), could it specifically have been Christ (or a *Christophany*) in the burning bush that spoke to Moses that day?

For you wonderful Bereans, let's continue to follow the path of verification set for us in the Scriptures so that we can see with more clarity… into the *Logos* Himself! It's all about His name!

There on Mt. Sinai, and out of the fiery *Presence* of God, the Lord announced to man His true name – a name for all generations to know. An extremely important and revealing name:

> *"Then Moses said to **God**, "Indeed when I come to the children of Israel and say to them, 'The God of your fathers has sent me to you,' and they say to me, 'What is His name?' what shall I say to them? And **God** said to Moses, "**I AM WHO I AM**." And He said, "Thus you shall say to the children of Israel, '**I AM** has sent me to you.'" (Exodus 3:13-14)*

What God was revealing in His name is that He *always* existed and will *always* exist. He is the *"uncreated One."* Names back in the Old Testament revealed much about the actual character and the substance of the person.

In revealing His name to Moses as the "**I AM**", the *"self-existent One,"* Ever-Present Helper, the Eternal God, He goes on to further reveal to Moses that He is not just revealing His name here… but the Lord is far more inferring **His Presence** with man! That is, His desire to dwell with man, and bring man into deeper worship unto Him!

Can this truly be a distinct *person* (singular) of the Godhead who is identifying Himself to Moses as the "**I AM**"? Yes! The Bible tells us which specific *person* of the Trinity was speaking that day from the midst of the fire – we see if from many other irrefutable portions of Scripture:

> "*Jesus said to them, "Truly, truly, I say to you,*
> *before Abraham was, **I am**. (ego eimi)" (John 8:58)*

Jesus was in the temple speaking to the chief leaders of Israel when He made that astonishing statement. He was declaring Diety before them and that **He** was the Eternal God that their fore–fathers knew; the God of Abraham, Isaac, and Jacob. The Pharisees were outraged at such a claim from Him because they knew He was identifying Himself as the **I AM** or Jehovah God of the Old Testament. The audacity of Jesus made the Pharisees so angry they picked up stones to hurl at Him.

But this is not an isolated incident either. Jesus *deliberately* echoes a pattern of themes that are unique to the name of Jehovah by repeatedly using the expression "**I AM**". The word in Greek for "**I AM**" is *ego eimi*. Let's take a closer look!

The high density of "**I AM**" sayings about Jehovah found in Chapters 40 thru 55 in the book of Isaiah clearly match the high density of "**I AM**" sayings of Jesus in the Gospel of John. The vast majority of the sayings found in Isaiah 40-55 point to the identity of Jehovah, whereas the theme of the Gospel of John is revealing the identity of Jesus. The Lord is brazenly claiming Himself to be Jehovah, by intentionally applying (quoting) the "language of Deity" to Himself from those chapters in Isaiah concerning the "**I AM**"! Jesus declares some 17 times in the book of John that He is the true "**I AM**".

If you see one elephant in a cloud, it may be a coincidence, but when you see 17 elephants in a row, all linked together trunk to tail, it is an unmistakable pattern of design! God is giving us *revelation* in the form of breadcrumbs to follow in the path of Scripture, all of it coming from the very Bread of Heaven Himself – Jesus Christ, the true **"I AM!"**

By itself **"I AM"** would prove little, but the pattern of His use in various themes in the book of John match exactly with Isaiah, and create an unmistakable mosaic that is a powerful and unmistakable proof of the Deity of Jesus Christ as **"I AM."**

The declarations from Jesus Christ are *distinct* and direct, yet grammatically many of the verses contain what we call a predicate nominative (from Koine Greek), meaning they are titles *of* Jesus - although they don't corroborate *who* Jesus is, they do define *what* Jesus is:

- *"**I Am** the Bread of Life."* (John 6:35)
- *"**I Am** the Light of the World."* (John 8:12)
- *"**I Am** the Door."* (John 10:9)
- *"**I Am** the Good Shepherd."* (John 10:11,14)
- *"**I Am** the Resurrection and the Life."* (John 11:25)
- *"**I Am** the Way and the Truth and the Life."* (John 14:6)
- *"**I Am** the Vine."* (John 15: 1, 5)

But to zero in on the abundance of substantive claims of Diety made by Jesus, the Gospel of John records Jesus speaking with a clear declaration that He is, in fact, the true **"I AM,"** only this time – <u>without using predicate nominatives</u>… meaning Jesus is not declaring *what* He is - but specifically *who* He is:

> *"**Jesus** said to them, "Truly, truly, I say to you,*
> *before Abraham was, **I Am**. (ego eimi)" (John 8:58)*

24

*"I said therefore to you, that you shall die in your sins; for unless you believe that **I Am**, (ego eimi) you shall die in your sins." (John 8:24)*

*"Jesus, therefore, said, 'When you lift up the Son of Man, then you will know that **I Am**.'" (ego eimi) (John 8:28)*

*"From now on I am telling you before it comes to pass, so that when it does occur, you may believe that **I Am**." (ego eimi) (John 13:19)*

*"The woman said to Him, 'I know that Messiah is coming.' (who is called Christ). 'When He comes, He will tell us all things.' Jesus said to her, '**I who speak to you I Am He**.'" (ego eimi) (John 4:25-26)*

*"Then, when they had rowed about three or four miles, they saw Jesus walking on the sea and drawing near to the boat, and they were frightened. But He said to them, 'Do not be afraid, **I Am He**.'" (ego eimi) (John 6:19-20)*

*"...Jesus said to them, '**I Am He**.' (ego eimi) And Judas, who betrayed Him, also stood with them. Now when He said to them, '**I am He**,' (ego emi) they drew back and fell to the ground." (John 18:5-6)*

*"Jesus answered, 'I have told you that **I Am He**.' (ego eimi) Therefore, if you seek Me, let these go their way." (John 18:8)*

Jesus is the great **"I AM!"** The Eternal God! Even John the Baptist declared Jesus to be the true, Eternal God:

*"This is He of whom I said <u>after</u> me cometh a Man which is preferred before me: for He was **before** me." (John 1:30)*

John was not referring to natural birth because John was conceived many months before Jesus. Remember John was born **before** Jesus… So when John said *"He was **before** me,"* John the Baptist was referring to Jesus as the *pre-existent* God!

There is a vast treasure of additional Scriptures validating the authenticity of Christ as being the **"I AM,"** and of Jesus being what the Bible refers to many times as the *"Angel of the Lord"* who guided Israel throughout the entire Old Testament!

As we continue to unfold these truths throughout this book, we will also see a distinct pattern emerge that conclusively links a direct association between Jesus Christ, the **I AM**, and the Holy Fire of God!

These *revelations* will be crucial for our study to grasp a deeper biblical understanding of the Manifest Presence of God upon the earth, as being the blazing, fiery, Son of God, Jesus Christ!

"BEFORE ABRAHAM WAS… I AM"

CHAPTER TWO
A CLOUD BY DAY
FIRE BY NIGHT

Chapter Two
A Cloud by Day – Fire by Night

From the midst of Holy Fire, the Eternal God, who now calls Himself the "**I AM**," commissioned Moses to go back to Egypt, to the house of bondage and decree "Let My People Go" to Pharaoh.

The Lord displayed many signs and wonders to Pharaoh and all of Egypt through plagues, but the heart of Pharaoh stubbornly refused to free the Hebrews until the tenth plague came, causing the death of the firstborn of all the Egyptians.

What a spectacle that great deliverance must have been – the Exodus of the children of God from not only the house of bondage – but from the most powerful nation on earth at the time, after some 400 years of slavery! God's people witnessed the incredible love and faithfulness of their Lord, in stunning fashion, through a powerful, and Divine intervention. They experienced some of the greatest displays of God's power ever seen on earth! Just to envision that company of people going out through the gates of Egypt under the power and Glory of God, carrying out the wealth of Egypt in vast amounts of gold, jewelry, and other costly treasures must have been awesome!

But even more fantastic was the fact that as they came out of the gates of Egypt, there appeared to them a visible cloud by day and a pillar of fire at night. Fire? Could that fire have been the same fire that first appeared to Moses on Mt. Sinai? Let's turn to the Bible and see what it says about that unusual event:

"And the __LORD__ went before them by day in a pillar of cloud to lead the way, and by night __in a pillar of fire__ to give them light, so as to go by day and night. He did not take away the pillar of cloud by day or the pillar of fire by night from before the people." (Exodus 13:21-22)

The Word of God gives us considerable reasons to believe that this Exodus, was being guided under a true *Christophany*! Can you just imagine the fiery Presence of Christ leading *"His first Church out into the Wilderness?"*

On top of that, the Lord *intentionally* led them away from the most common route that one would take towards their eventual destination – the land of Canaan.

"Then it came to pass when Pharaoh had let the people go, that God did not lead them by way of the land of the Philistines, although that was near; for God said, 'Lest perhaps the people change their minds when they see war and return to Egypt.' So God led the people around by way of the wilderness of the Red Sea." (Exodus 13:17-18)

Do you believe this pillar of fire was the pre-incarnate Christ, leading His Church out into the Wilderness towards the land of Canaan? The Apostle Paul *clearly* said __it was Christ__ leading them. As Paul was discussing how the children of Israel's' hearts were continually murmuring along the journey in the wilderness, Paul said that the Manifest Presence of God in the Cloud by Day and Fire by Night __to whom they complained__ was none other than Jesus Christ!

"Nor let us tempt __Christ, as some of them also tempted__, and were destroyed by serpents;" (1 Corinthians 10:9, Numbers 21:6)

The Apostle Paul further confirms that __it was truly Christ__:

"Moreover, brethren, I do not want you to be unaware that all our fathers were under the cloud; all passed through the sea, all

were baptized into Moses in the cloud and in the sea, all ate the
same spiritual food and all drunk the same spiritual drink. For
they drank of that spiritual Rock that followed them,
and that Rock was Christ!!! *(1 Corinthians 10:1-4)*

The Word of God delivers even more ample evidence that it was, in fact, Christ Himself leading His Church forth – out from the gates of Egypt toward the Promised Land (Canaan) ina glorious and fiery Presence – as the beautiful Shekinah Glory of God shone on them! Behold the King of Kings, Jesus Christ, the mighty Deliverer of Israel!

"I will surely assemble all of you, O Jacob,
I will surely gather the remnant of Israel;
I will put them together like sheep of the fold,
Like a flock in the midst of their pasture;
They shall make a loud noise because of so many people.
The One who breaks open will come up before them;
They will break out, pass through the gate,
And go out by it; **_their King will pass before them_**,
With the L__ORD__ **_at their head_**.*" (Micah 2:12-13)*

The Cloud by Day and Fire by Night (Christ), led His people directly towards the Sea of Reeds (Red Sea) so that they became butted up against the wall of the sea when behind them came the sudden sound of Pharaoh's armies, chariots, and riders. There was no physical way of escape for the children of Israel. They were forced to decide what to do; either surrender, fight the Egyptian armies or – to place all their trust in God!

Though God was there in their midst to lead and protect them, the people chose to murmur before Moses and before God:

"Is this not the word that we told you in Egypt, saying,
'Let us alone that we may serve the Egyptians'? For it would

31

have been better for us to serve the Egyptians than that we should die in the wilderness." (Exodus 14:12)

Moses assured the frightened and agitated people what the Lord God (Christ) would do for them in that moment of peril:

And Moses said to the people, "Do not be afraid. Stand still, and see the __Salvation__ of the LORD, which He will accomplish for you today. For the Egyptians whom you see today, you shall see again no more forever. __The LORD will fight for you__, and you shall hold your peace." (Exodus 14:13-14).

What Moses declared to the people at that moment was astonishing! When he declared that they would see the *"Salvation"* of the Lord – that very word in Hebrew was *yeshuw'ah* from which we derive Yeshua (literally Jesus Christ), so better said, Moses was declaring *"Stand still and see **Jesus** your God move on your behalf!"* How awesome is that?

But how would the Lord fight for them? Jesus did an amazing thing, as the *"**Angel of the Lord**,"* He moved before them, and then went around behind them in Cloud Presence. He formed a *"**wall of fire**"* between them and the Egyptian army. On the Israelites side of the wall, it was the fiery Presence of Christ producing light for them to see clearly, but on the other side of the wall - Pharaoh's armies experienced darkness. Why would the Lord do this for His chosen people? Throughout the Old Testament the Lord repeatedly demonstrated to Israel both His Love and His protection:

"… the Glory of the LORD shall be your rear guard." (Isaiah 58:8)

"For __I__, says the LORD, '__will be a wall of fire__ all around her, and I will be the Glory in her midst.'" (Zechariah 2:5)

Thus, the children of Israel experienced the most incredible deliverance ever recorded in history as they passed through the Red Sea, which had parted from them, and they passed over on dry ground! The fiery Presence of Christ continued to lead His Church into the Wilderness – as a Cloud by Day and Fire by Night! Christ led them to His Holy Mountain called Mt. Sinai!

*"O God, when **You** went out before Your people When You marched through the wilderness, Selah. The earth shook; the heavens also dropped rain at the Presence of God; Sinai itself was moved at the Presence of God, the God of Israel." (Psalms 68:7-8)*

We have presented a weight (preponderance) of Scripture as evidence that it was truly Christ who met Moses that day in the burning bush. It was also Christ, being the distinct *person* of the Godhead who was manifested to Israel as a Cloud by Day and Fire by Night, leading His Church out of Egypt towards the Promised Land. It is not hard to believe that it was also Christ who manifested Himself to Abraham on the mountain of Covenant (Mt. Hermon) who passed through the sacrifices in such fiery Presence!

It would bode well for us in our study on the Holy Fire of God to try and gain an even greater understanding concerning the many other highly possible *Christophanies*, in the Old Testament that (identified through a specific vernacular) commonly referred to Christ as the *"Angel of the Lord."*

So, let's *"follow the Fire"* of Christ through the Old Testament! As we do, we will begin to see Truth and an unmistakable association unfold between these three things:

A. The distinct *person* of Christ in manifestation

B. The Angel of the Lord

C. The appearance of Holy Fire

THE SENT SON

Before we go any further, I believe there is a question that needs to be asked. Of the three in one Godhead, that is, the Father, Son, and Holy Spirit, why would Jesus be the *One* (singular tense) *person* of the Godhead chosen to come into earthly realms in both manifestations throughout the Old Testament and as the promised Messiah in the New Testament?

For the real answer to that question, we must go back… not just back *into* time - but back *before* time itself!

Somewhere in eternity past (before the foundation of the world was laid), the counsel of the Godhead conceived a purpose. Paul called it God's *eternal purpose* in the book of Ephesians.

That purpose was that God wanted a family that He could impart His very own life, meaning His Divine life, into a creature that was not yet even created, and that this creature would share His life and make it *visible*. So, the Godhead began creation with this purpose in mind. God created the invisible realm, and then God created the visible realm.

And God created all these things **_by_** His Son. He created all things **_through_** His Son and (most importantly), He created all things **_for_** His Son! All things were created by Him, through Him, and for Him. All for Jesus Christ – the Son of God!

> "*He* (Christ) *is the* (manifest) *image of the invisible God,*
> *the firstborn over all creation. <u>For by Him all things were*
> *created</u> that are in Heaven and that are on earth, visible and*

34

invisible, whether thrones or dominions or principalities or powers. <u>All things were created through Him and for Him</u>.
(Colossians 1:15-16)

Jesus Christ, the Son, is the centrality of the purpose of God, the Father. So, God takes this purpose that He has developed in His heart in eternity past, and He shrouds it in a mystery, and then He hides it in His Son.

"...the mystery which has been hidden from ages and from generations, but now has been revealed to His saints." (Colossians 1:26)

Then God creates a beautiful garden in the midst of the visible realm and forms man from His very own image and breathes life into him, so man became a *living soul.*

This created man, called Adam, was destined to be the *eternal companion* (Bride) to God the Son, and part of the Royal Family of God. But Adam, along with his created wife Eve disobeyed the orders of God and ate from one of the two trees in the garden they were told not to eat from, or they would surely *die.*

At the fall of man, God saw His creation morph into an enemy, an enemy of God. But God through His *infinite wisdom,* and Love, (knowing beforehand that man would fall) – had already made provision through His eternal plan to restore man back to right relationship with Him.

God chose a man named Abram, and through him created a great nation called Israel. God's plan was to restore all things back to a right relationship with Him through Israel, but unfortunately, Israel failed.

So, God ended up doing the unthinkable! The Eternal God Himself, God the Father, sent God the Son, Jesus Christ, right into the embodiment of His creation, and God the Son stepped into time and became a man.

Once upon the earth, the Son of God paid the ultimate price for sin, taking upon Himself the curse of all sin and death that fallen man had incurred — just as God said it would. Then Christ died a substitutionary death (in our place) on the cross, a death that atoned for our sins once and for all.

Jesus paid the ultimate sacrifice for our inevitable death sentence and the wrath of God that would have been poured out upon each one of us. He did it willingly, through His very blood, out of great Love for all men. No greater Love has ever been demonstrated in this earth!

Jesus Christ is "**The Sent Son**!" From eternity, then down through Old Testament Scripture in various visitations, and types and shadows, *everything* points to Christ and Him alone.

Then the fullness of His Glory was revealed to us when Jesus became man and was born as the Saviour of the world, the Messiah, in the city of Bethlehem, as the prophets foretold. Jesus, the beautiful Son of God, was *sent* to us, from the Father.

"But when the fullness of the time had come,
God __sent__ forth His Son (Galatians 4:4)

"For God so loved the world He __sent__ His Son…" (John 3:16)

"For I have come down from Heaven, not to do My own will,
but the will of Him who __sent__ Me." (John 6:38)

"…But I know Him, for I am from Him, and He __sent__ Me." (John 7:29)

"I am One who bears witness of Myself and the Father
*who **sent** Me bears witness of Me." (John 8:18)*

Since everything was created by Him, through Him and for Him, to the delight of His Father, is it any wonder that we see the very **sent** Son of God in manifestation across the Old Testament before His incarnation at Bethlehem in the New Testament?

When we begin to understand the totality of God the Father's eternal purpose, being expressed through and for His Son, a beautiful picture emerges across the canvas of time. It was **Christ, the Sent Son** making Covenant with Abram (unto Himself). It was Christ, the Eternal **I AM** revealing Himself (and His Father's purpose) to Moses on Mt. Sinai. It was Christ in the Cloud by Day and Pillar of Fire by Night leading His First Church through the wilderness towards the Promised Land and to the eventual fulfillment of His ultimate plan of reconciling man back to God by death on a cross at Mt. Calvary!

Christ is the visible *person* of the Godhead seen upon the earth! It was Jesus Christ who was visibly working out the complete will of God upon the earth throughout both the Old and New Testaments! Christ, the complete personification of His Father!

"He is the image (visible) of the invisible God,
the firstborn over all creation." (Colossians 1:15)

"...who being the brightness of His glory and the express image
(visible) of His person (The Father) ..." (Hebrews 1:3)

As we said, the Lord appeared many times to Israel in the Old Testament through a metaphor described as *"The Angel of the Lord, or The Angel of the Covenant."*

This type of *language* referring to Christ caused confusion for many because not all manifestations of *"The Angel of the Lord"* were God Himself, but were actually heavenly beings sent as messengers *from* God.

> *"And of the angels, He says: "Who makes His angels spirits*
> *And His ministers a flame of fire." (Hebrews 1:7)*

From this, we can determine that in some instances *"the Angel of the Lord"* was the pre-incarnate Christ, while at other times in Old Testament history, a reference *"the Angel of the Lord"* could be used to refer to heavenly beings sent by God to fulfill a purpose in the earth.

It would be expedient to apply the rule of *context* when attempting to determine such Scripture that refers to *"the Angel of the Lord,"* as to whether it refers to the pre-incarnate Christ or a Holy Angel sent by God. By the specific context, we mean looking at the entire storyline of Scripture concerning each manifestation, looking for claims or functions of Deity in either the words or works of what *"Angel of the Lord"* is referenced.

It is important to note that the literal word "Angel" does not just mean "winged creature." At its core etymology, it means "Messenger, Envoy, Ambassador." One who is *sent* by God!

In instances where *"the Angel of the Lord"* was a *Christophany,* — the Lord was fulfilling a purpose in the earth as a sent Envoy or Ambassador of the Father, coming as **The Sent Son**!

The reason the distinction between the two is so important to our study is that almost all of the appearances of *"the Angel of the Lord"* that have been identified as highly probable Christophanies, and these were clearly associated with the manifestation of Holy Fire—the very Fire of God!

JESUS CHRIST

THE ANGEL OF THE LORD

ANGEL OF THE COVENANT

CHAPTER 3
HOLY FIRE
ON MT. SINAI

Chapter 3
Holy Fire On Mt. Sinai

The Lord was very intentional concerning His plans for the children of Israel, whom He led out of Egypt. He had planned to bring them up to His Holy Mountain called Mt. Sinai or Mt. Horeb, for them to worship Him on that mountain.

"So He said, "I will certainly be with you. And this shall be a sign to you that I have sent you: when you have brought the people out of Egypt, you shall worship God on this mountain." (Exodus 3:12)

In the third month after leaving Egypt, Moses led them to the very mountain where He had encountered the "**I AM**." As they camped at the base of that mountain, Moses went up to meet with God. The Lord spoke to Moses from that mountain and revealed His precious heart (plan) for these people.

"Thus you shall say to the house of Jacob, and tell the children of Israel: 'You have seen what I did to the Egyptians, and how I <u>bore you on eagles' wings and brought you to Myself</u>. Now therefore, if you will indeed obey My voice and keep My covenant, then <u>you shall be a special treasure to Me</u> above all people; for all the earth is Mine. And <u>you shall be to Me a Kingdom of Priests</u> and <u>a holy nation</u>.' These are the words which you shall speak to the children of Israel." (Exodus 19:3-6)

Moses gathered the elders of the people and shared with them what the Lord had spoken to him. How awesome that must have been for them to learn what was in God's heart for them!

Then the Lord spoke to Moses again, telling him that He was going to appear before all the peoples in a thick cloud so that all of Israel could audibly hear the voice of God as He spoke to Moses so that they might believe Moses from that point on.

The Lord instructed Moses to consecrate the people for two days, including washing their clothes, etc. in order to be prepared to meet with the Lord on the third day. The Lord said that on that day He would appear on Mt. Sinai to all the people!

The Lord also issued a very stern warning for the people not to touch the mountain in any way – or they would surely be put to death! The Lord said that when they heard the long blast of the trumpet (shofar) on the third day, they were then to approach closer to the base of the mountain.

On the third day, the most incredible thing began to happen… There were great flashes of lightning and rolls of thunder upon Mt. Sinai, and then a thick cloud began to appear over the mountain. Suddenly there was a loud blast of a trumpet, from the Lord Himself, and the people greatly trembled!

Then Moses brought the frightened people even closer to the mountain, which by now had become completely covered in smoke. Then the Lord God descended upon the mountain in Holy Fire Presence! As He did, the entire mountain quaked greatly! (He can't help it - He's God!)

The whole nation saw the awesome Presence of God, manifested as Fire on the Mountain! Then Moses was called up the mountain again by God and told to warn the people not to come any closer to gaze at the awesome God - lest they perish! This was Holy Ground, for the Manifest Presence was upon the mountain, and the mountain burned with Holy Fire!

The people were so terrified of the Manifest Presence of God that they stood afar off and begged Moses:

> *"You speak with us, and we will hear, but let not God*
> *speak with us, lest we die; and Moses said to the people,*
> *"Do not fear; for God has come to test you, and that His fear*
> *may be before you, so that you may not sin." So the people*
> *stood afar off, but Moses drew near the thick darkness*
> *where God was." (Exodus 20:19-21)*

The Glory of the Lord rested upon Mt. Sinai that day, as God gave Moses instructions and laws to help govern the children of Israel. On the seventh day, the Lord called Moses to come up even higher into His thick, cloud Presence. The Bible says:

> *"The sight of the glory of the LORD was like a <u>consuming fire</u>*
> *on the top of the mountain in the eyes of the children of Israel. So*
> *Moses went into the midst of the cloud and went up into the*
> *mountain. And Moses was on the mountain forty days and*
> *forty nights." (Exodus 24:17, 18)*

In Deuteronomy, when Moses is talking to the children of Israel, preparing them to move forward in their journey towards Canaan, the vernacular Moses used to describe to them who the Lord is, was clearly akin to Holy Fire!

> *"Then you came near and stood at the foot of the mountain,*
> *and the mountain burned with fire to the midst of heaven, with*
> *darkness, cloud, and thick darkness. And the LORD spoke to you*
> *out of <u>the midst of the fire</u>. You heard the sound of the words, but*
> *saw no form; you only heard a voice." (Deuteronomy 4:11, 12)*

"Did any people ever hear the voice of God speaking out of <u>the</u> <u>midst of the fire</u>, as you have heard, and live?" (Deuteronomy 4:33)

"Out of heaven He let you hear His voice, that He might instruct you; on earth, <u>He showed you His great fire</u>, and you heard His words out of the midst of the fire." (Deuteronomy 4:36)

"Therefore understand today that the LORD your God is He who goes over before you <u>as a consuming fire</u>. He will destroy them and bring them down before you; so you shall drive them out and destroy them quickly, as the LORD has said to you." (Deuteronomy 9:3)

───❦───

What an amazing journey thus far! Let's recount... The Holy Fire of the **"I AM"** appears to Moses upon Mt. Sinai, and it turns out to be none other than Christ Himself who was speaking from the midst of the burning bush. He commissions Moses to go to Egypt and deliver His people with great signs and wonders!

Then the children of Israel come out of Egypt under the same fiery Presence of God that Moses experienced on Mt. Sinai! This pillar of fire was the fiery Presence of Christ leading His first Church into the wilderness - back towards Mt. Sinai so that they could worship Him there upon that mountain!

Along the way, the Egyptian army comes after them and has them trapped against the sea – but God comes as a literal "wall of fire" between them and the Egyptians, to protect them!

Then Moses declares "Behold the Jesus (Salvation) of the Lord," as Christ parts the waters and His first church in the wilderness pass through the waters in a symbolic baptism.

Then the fiery Presence of Christ leads His nation to the Holy Mountain. God then calls forth Moses and tells him His plan to provide the children of Israel with a Covenant.

Jesus offers these very people to be His special treasure, as a Kingdom of Priests – so long as they agree to obey His commands. The children of Israel accept the offer (though they hadn't even heard the terms of it yet!)

To do this in stunning display – God plans to reveal His Manifest Presence with visible Fire and Glory all over the entire mountain! He is going to hold a special audience with Moses and let all the children of Israel "listen in" so they will believe God's intentions, and obey both God and Moses.

Then God shows up in spectacular form on the mountain in Holy Fire! With astounding special effects; including lightning, thunder, an enveloping thick cloud Presence. There were trumpet blasts and earthquakes! God is on His mountain!

God begins to speak from the very fire that is now engulfing the entire mountain! The people are so absolutely undone by the awesomeness of this, they plead with Moses to be excused, asking Moses to *hear* what else God would say and then pledged to follow Moses in whatever was requested by God.

Moses continues to listen audibly to the majestic voice of God, and God begins to give Moses all the laws. At the end of the giving of the laws, God ends the encounter by offering these incredible promises and exhortations:

> *"Behold, **I send an Angel** before you to keep you in the way*
> *and to bring you into the place which I have prepared. **Beware***
> ***of Him** and **obey His voice; do not provoke Him**, for **He will***

__not pardon your transgressions;__ for __My name is in Him__. But if you indeed __obey His voice__ and do all that __I speak__, then I will be an enemy to your enemies and an adversary to your adversaries. __For My Angel__ will go before you and bring you into the Amorites and the Hittites and the Perizzites and the Canaanites and the Hivites and the Jebusites; and I will cut them off. You shall not bow down to their gods, nor serve them, nor do according to their works, but you shall utterly overthrow them and completely break down their sacred pillars.

"So you shall <u>serve the LORD your God</u>, and <u>He</u> will bless your bread and your water. And I will take sickness away from the midst of you. No one shall suffer miscarriage or be barren in your land; I will fulfill the number of your days.

"I will send My fear before you; I will cause confusion among all the people to whom you come, and will make all your enemies turn their backs to you. And I will send hornets before you, which shall drive out the Hivite, the Canaanite, and the Hittite from before you. I will not drive them out from before you in one year, lest the land become desolate and the beasts of the field become too numerous for you. Little by little I will drive them out from before you, until you have increased, and you inherit the land. And I will set your bounds from the Red Sea to the sea, Philistia, and from the desert to the River. For I will deliver the inhabitants of the land into your hand, and you shall drive them out before you. You shall make no covenant with them, nor with their gods. They shall not dwell in your land, lest they make you sin against Me. For if you serve their gods, it will surely be a snare to you." (Exodus 23:20-33)

Did you catch that? It is astonishing what was just spoken by our God! *"Behold, **I** send... **My Angel**!"*

You must understand that this is being spoken in *first person* context. The actual person speaking is declaring that He would send **His** Angel... This is a dynamic revelation! There are two questions that must be asked here!

Question # 1. Who exactly is the "**He**" speaking?
Question # 2. Who is the "**My Angel**" that "**He**" is sending?

I believe the fascinating mystery can best be understood by answering the second question – first...

Revered Bible scholars say that this is none other than *"**The Angel of the Covenant**."* These sensible Bible expositors identify the "**Him**" as the second person of the Trinity, the Ever-Blessed Son of God! The attribute given this Angel is clearly in the line of Deity.

> A. *"He will not pardon your transgressions"* (No messenger Angel ever was given that right – only God Himself).
> B. *"My name is in Him"* (Ascribing Deity to this Angel).
> C. *"So you shall serve the Lord your God, and He will Bless you"* (Referring to the Angel "as God" who is to lead them).

This Angel of the Lord was **Christ**, the "**Sent Son**" of God**, the Angel of the Covenant**, sent to lead the children of Israel into Canaan. Later, Isaiah beautifully describes this Angel of God:

> *"In all their affliction He was afflicted, and the*
> *Angel of His Presence saved them; in His love and*
> *in His pity He redeemed them, and He bore them and*
> *carried them all the days of old." (Isaiah 63:9)*

Malachi referred to Christ, the Angel of the Covenant as *"The Messenger of the Covenant"* who would come. In the book of Hebrews, we get an even clearer picture of Christ, when He is referred to as "Jesus, the **_Mediator_** of the New Covenant."

Would you not think it safe to believe that the "Angel of the Covenant" is Christ Himself? If not, then I challenge you to do a deeper study on - *the Angel of the Covenant.* It is a fascinating topic and revelatory study that will open up the depths of the mystery of Christ!

If you are convinced, that the Angel of the Covenant is Christ, then let's go back to the first question - for it becomes quite clear who was audibly speaking to Moses and the children of Israel on Mt. Sinai that day… God, The Father!

Who else had the authority or right to commission the Son of God to the role and purpose of the **Angel of the Covenant**? There is an enormous amount of Scripture throughout the Bible where Jesus repeatedly declares that He has been *"sent"* (commissioned) by His Father!

Let's try to get this in perspective, and look at an overview of what just happened on Mt. Sinai during this incredible encounter between God and man.

The Godhead themselves, (that is the three-in-one Living God or Trinity), is about to fulfill their purpose and plan, which they had ordained from *before* the foundation of the earth. That through a Covenant promised to Abraham; they would deliver his offspring from the house of bondage (Egypt) and bring them to the Holy Mountain where the Godhead would reveal to all of Israel even more of the Holy Covenant that God was committed to establishing with the nation of Israel.

The Godhead setup an incredible theater on Mt. Sinai to introduce the Covenant to them there. The people were given instructions on how to cleanse themselves and be fully prepared to meet with the Godhead and receive the Covenant.

Then the awesome and majestic Presence of the <u>entire</u> Godhead descends upon the mountain! God, the Father, is about to speak to the entire nation of Israel. But because it is God the Father present on the mountain, the Godhead gives the people the highest level of warning NOT to touch the mountain, or they would die. Even more so - they are directed NOT to try and get to advantage point to try and "gaze" upon God the Father – because nobody can see God the Father and live – isn't this what Scripture says?

> *"Not that anyone has seen the Father, except He who is from God; He has seen the Father." (John 6:46)*

> *"But He said, "You cannot see My face; for no man shall see Me, and live." (Exodus 33:20)*

> *"And the LORD said to Moses, "Go down and warn the people, lest they break through to gaze at the LORD, and many of them perish." (Exodus 19:21)*

Thunderings begin to rumble on the mountain and lightning begin to light the dark sky. Then a thick cloud Presence began to cover Mt. Sinai, as one person of the Godhead releases a mighty blast from a trumpet, which sounded long and became louder and louder. Do you think this could have been the Son of God announcing His Father?

Then on that Holy Mountain, the precious Godhead began to give forth Their Covenant to the nation of Israel. First to all the people, and then the rest to Moses after the people became frightened from the fire and of the Voice coming *out* of the fire.

Then the distinct person of the Godhead, the Father, speaks and declares **He** is sending **His Angel** (Christ) to be Israel's Guide, Provider, Protector, Avenger, and Healer! The Father declares **He** is giving them the Promised land – the entire land between the Red Sea and the Mediterranean on the one hand and the Desert and the Euphrates River on the other. All of this - if they will obey **His Angel's** Voice!

It would not be the last time that the Father of the Godhead would speak audibly to the children of Israel and encourage them to listen and follow **His Son, Jesus!** In the New Testament, the Father did the same!

"While He was still speaking, behold, a bright cloud overshadowed them; and suddenly a voice came out of the cloud, saying, "This is My Beloved Son, in whom I am well pleased. Hear Him!" (Matthew 17:5)

HOLY FIRE ON MT. SINAI

CHAPTER FOUR
ALTARS OF FIRE

Chapter Four
Altars Of Fire

From the very first moment that Adam and Eve disobeyed God, and ate of the fruit that the Lord told them not to eat of, death entered the human race, just as the Lord said:

> *"Then the LORD God took the man and put him in the garden*
> *of Eden to tend and keep it. And the LORD God commanded the*
> *man, saying, "Of every tree of the garden you may freely eat; but*
> *of the tree of the knowledge of good and evil, you shall not eat, for in*
> *the day that you eat of it you shall surely die." (Genesis 2:15-17)*

After Adam and Eve had sinned by eating the fruit, the Lord did an unusual thing... He covered both Adam and Eve in animal skins as a covering (even though He was banishing them from the Garden of Eden). God didn't just place animal skins on them as clothing to stay warm, this was a symbolic type, and shadow of *covering* that would end up speaking throughout the Bible about sacrifice, substitutionary death and the shedding of blood for the forgiveness of sin.

"...without shedding of blood there is no remission." (Hebrews 9:22)

Thus, began a downward spiral of mankind. About 1100 years beyond Adam, man had become so corrupted that God decided to flood the earth. Why did God flood the earth? Genesis 6 tells you why:

    A. The wickedness of men had become great... *verse 5*
    B. Every imagination/thought of man was evil... *verse 5*
    C. The earth was filled with violence... *verse 11*

D. All flesh had become corrupt… *verse* 12

During those days, there was a righteous man named Noah, a just man, who walked with God and was a preacher of righteousness. God commissioned Noah to build an Ark. He gave Noah the exact blueprints (details) on how to build it.

God's mercy was just as evident at the time of the flood as His judgment, for the people of the land had an opportunity to come into that Ark – even though they chose not to!

The amazing thing about the building of this Ark, was *how* God told Noah to build it:

> *"Make yourself an Ark of gopherwood; make rooms in the Ark, and* **cover** *it inside and outside with* **pitch**.*" (Genesis 6:14)*

The word in Hebrew used here for "pitch" is the word "*kaphar*" which means *atonement*. It is the root word of *kippur* from which we get *yom kippur,* meaning the Day of Atonement.

So, the pitch that Noah used as a *covering* inside and out of the Ark was somehow tied to atonement, meaning the pitch must have somehow had blood and sacrifice associated with it. Can you see the beautiful picture emerge of the type and shadow of Christ inviting a fallen world to escape judgment and come to Him, the Ark of Safety?

God was just beginning to teach man about covering, atonement, the shedding of blood, sacrifice, substitutionary death, etc. It was the beginning of a scarlet thread that God would weave all the way through the entire Old Testament, and then bring that scarlet thread right up to the cross of Christ on Mt. Calvary in the New Testament!

There is a direct association throughout the Old Testament between altars that men built unto the Lord and the offering of sacrifices unto God in blood atonement. You can see it as early as Genesis 4 with Cain and Abel. The book of Hebrews says:

> "By faith, Abel offered to God a more excellent **sacrifice** than Cain, through which he obtained witness that he was righteous, God testifying of his gifts, and through it he being dead still speaks."
> (Hebrews 11:4)

The word "**sacrifice**" used in that portion of Scripture, is the same word used for an animal sacrifice unto the Lord. The Bible also says that Noah built an altar and offered *burnt* sacrifices unto the Lord as did Abram, Isaac, Jacob, Job and many others.

In Exodus 24, at the ratification of the Covenant, Moses built an altar at the base of Mt. Sinai and offered *burnt* sacrifices up to the Lord. Then he took the blood and sprinkled it on the altar and the people declaring:

> "This is the blood of the covenant which the LORD has made with you according to all these words." (Exodus 24:8)

Why is this important to our study? Because just as there is a direct link between altars and sacrifices, there is also a direct connection between sacrifices and fire… including Holy Fire!

Moses instructed Aaron and the newly formed Levitical priests that the fire burning on the altar must *never* go out. This was to be a significant part their priestly roles and function.

*"Then the LORD spoke to Moses, saying, "Command Aaron and
his sons, saying, 'This is the law of the burnt offering: The burnt
offering shall be on the hearth upon the altar all night until morning,
and the fire of the altar shall be kept burning on it... 'A fire shall always
be burning on the altar; it shall never go out.'" (Leviticus 6:8,9,13)*

Then something amazing happened! The priests were
commanded by Moses to present the sacrifice offerings on the
altar – but one day became, unlike any other day the children
of Israel (who were all present) had ever experienced!

*"Then Aaron lifted his hand toward the people, blessed them,
and came down from offering the sin offering, the burnt offering,
and peace offerings. And Moses and Aaron went into the tabernacle
of the meeting, and came out and blessed the people. Then the glory of
the LORD appeared to all the people, **and fire came out from before
the LORD and consumed the burnt offering and the fat on the altar**.
When all the people saw it, they shouted and fell on their faces."*
(Leviticus 9:22-24)

The Holy Fire of God came down and consumed the sacrifice!
Man learned first-hand here that their God is a consuming fire
and that His fire is Holy Fire!

For the Bible says in the very next chapter of Leviticus that
Nadab and Abihu, who were sons of Aaron brought their
censers, put fire on them, sprinkled them with incense, and
then tried to offer it up to the Lord. But this time, the fire of God
came forth and devoured both of them, killing them. Why?

Because the Word of God said, they offered up *"profane"* fire
unto the Lord, that was something outside of God's instruction
and ordinance. But exactly what was *profane* fire? The Bible also
refers to it as *"strange fire."*

In Hebrew, the word is *"zuwr,"* and it means;

A. Stranger. Foreigner.
B. Adulterous. Prostitute. Harlot.
C. Estranged. Alienated.

They came before the Lord pretentiously and tried to offer up something **unholy**. We can see through this story that the Holy Fire of God can come in blessing and consume an acceptable sacrifice or it can come in judgment and devour!

Nadab and Abihu weren't the only ones that offered *profane* fire to the Lord and ended up being consumed. The Bible says that because of the rebellion of Korah and his company that:

> *"A fire came out from the LORD and consumed the two hundred and fifty men who were offering incense." (Numbers 16:35)*

Wow! How many times have we come into the House of God and perhaps offered up *unholy* fire unto the Lord i.e. when we were distant (estranged) from the Lord at the time... perhaps harboring secret sin in our life (not dealt with) yet trying to offer up to God *phileo* fire (human passion) instead of *agape* fire?

> *"These people draw near to Me with their mouth,*
> *and honor Me with their lips, but their heart is far from Me."*
> *(Matthew 15:8)*

The Lord will not despise a broken (repentant) and contrite heart. When you call upon the Lord, He comes and cleanses you by His Holy Blood, and with His Fire! He alone can purify our hearts!

> *"For He is like a refiner's fire, and like launderers' soap.*
> *He will sit as a refiner and a purifier of silver; He will*
> *purify the sons of Levi, and purge them as gold and*

*silver that they may offer the LORD an offering in
righteousness." (Malachi 3:2,3)*

*"The refining pot is for silver and the furnace for gold,
But the LORD assays the hearts." (Proverbs 17:3)*

Think of it, the very Fire of God filled your heart when you
were baptized in His Love since you are now priests of the
Most High God, you need to keep His Holy Fire burning on the
altar of your heart - day and night, remembering:

*"The LORD, your God, is a consuming fire,
a jealous God." (Deuteronomy 4:24)*

The Brazen Altar

The root word of "altar" in Hebrew means *"to slay, or
slaughter."* The brazen altar or bronze altar represented
judgment upon the sins of Israel.

The brazen altar was the place for offering a burnt sacrifice
unto the Lord. The brazen altar stood in the outer courtyard of
the Tabernacle tent, representing the first steps that sinful man
must take in attempting to approach the Holy Presence of God
that was inside the Tabernacle tent – man *first* had to be
cleansed by the blood (sacrifice) of an innocent creature.

For a sin offering, a person would bring an unblemished, male
animal to the priest at the Tabernacle gate. The person would
then lay his hand upon the head of the animal, identifying his
sin and guilt was being transferred from himself to the animal.

*"He is to lay his hand on the head of the burnt offering, and it will be
accepted on his behalf to make atonement for him." (Leviticus 1:4)*

Then the priest would slaughter the animal, burn the sacrifice and pour the blood on the bottom of the altar. The shedding of blood was the only acceptable act for the *atonement* of sin and cleansing in the Old Testament.

> *"For the life of a creature is in the blood, and I have given it to you to make atonement for yourselves on the altar; it is the blood that makes atonement for one's life." (Leviticus 17:11)*

The brazen altar stood raised up on a mound of earth, *higher* than the surrounding furniture. Likewise, this was a type and shadow of Christ, our sacrifice, who was put on a piece of wood (cross), that was set up on a mound… that mound called Mt. Calvary. It's important to understand **Golgotha was an altar**! It was the slaughter place of Christ! The Holy Sacrifice unto God on behalf of all people.

Until Christ, the substitutionary death of the animal paid the mandatory price for sin, the shedding of the blood covered the sin, and the burning of the sacrifice *consumed* the offering.

Sometimes the fire on the altar was generated by man and sometimes by God! But in the Old Testament, this wasn't the only altar of fire!

The Altar of Incense

There was yet another altar of fire in the Tabernacle tent. It was the golden Altar of Incense which was in the Holy Place, right before the curtain that separated the Holy Place from the Holy of Holies.

It was made of acacia wood and overlaid with pure gold. Four horns protruded from the four corners of the altar. God commanded the priests to burn the incense every morning and evening (at the same time the daily burnt offerings were made).

The incense was to be left burning continually throughout the day and evening as a pleasing fragrance to the Lord. It was made from 4 equal parts of precious spices; stacte, onycha, galbanum, and frankincense. It was considered Holy.

God commanded the Israelites not to use the same formula outside of the Tabernacle to make perfume for their own consumption, lest they are cut off from their people.

The incense was a representation of prayer and intercession for the people being lifted to God as a sweet aroma. God wanted His dwelling to be a place where people could approach Him and pray to Him.

> "…for my house will be called a house of
> prayer for all nations." (Isaiah 56:7)

Can you picture the fragrance of intercession being raised to the Lord, like fire burning on the Altar of Incense? We get a glimpse of it from the sweet psalmist of Israel (King David):

> "May my prayer be set before you like incense; may the lifting
> up of my hands be like the evening sacrifice." (Psalm 141:2)

Even the Lord Jesus Christ, who is our great High Priest continually flows in fiery intercession for us unto His Father:

> "But He, because He continues forever, has an unchangeable
> priesthood. Therefore He is also able to save to the uttermost
> those who come to God through Him, since He always lives to
> make intercession for them." (Hebrews 7:24, 25)

In the New Testament, our hearts became a part of the Altar of Incense. For intercession is made deep within the recesses of the heart. We don't even know how to properly move in this intercession by ourselves, so the Holy Spirit comes and *generates* intercession deep inside us:

> *"Likewise the Spirit also helps in our weaknesses. For we do not know what we should pray for as we ought, but the Spirit Himself makes intercession for us with groanings which cannot be uttered. Now He who searches the hearts knows what the mind of the Spirit is because He makes intercession for the saints according to the will of God." (Romans 8:26, 27*

What is so amazing is that the golden Altar of Incense in the Tabernacle was a *pattern* of that which exists in Heaven! The intercession from our hearts fills golden bowls of incense in Heaven. Then when God instructs, the fire of God from the altar ignites the prayers of the saints like incense that ascends to God. God seems to honor the sweet incense, and then He casts it back to earth in the form of answered prayer!

> *"Then another angel, having a golden censer, came and stood at the altar. He was given much incense, that he should offer it with the prayers of all the saints upon the golden altar which was before the throne. And the smoke of the incense, with the prayers of the saints, ascended before God from the angel's hand. Then the angel took the censer, filled it with fire from the altar, and threw it to the earth. And there were noises, thunderings, lightning and an earthquake." (Revelation 8:3-5)*

What an incredible vision of our God! The Lord comes and *consumes* acceptable sacrifices on one altar - as well as our prayers and intercessions on another altar - with His Holy Fire!

The Angel of the Lord (Christ) appeared to the barren wife of Manoah and told her she would conceive a son, and that she was to drink no wine which could have harmed her baby during pregnancy. The "man of God" also told her that her son would be a Nazarite from the womb and help deliver Israel out of the hand of the Philistines.

She was so amazed by this encounter that she ran and told her husband Manoah what had happened. Manoah prayed unto the Lord that He would bring this "Man of God" back so He could teach them what they must do for the child who would be born to them.

When the Angel of the Lord appeared again to the wife, Manoah was not there, so she ran and got her husband. When Manoah saw the Angel, he said to Him "Are you the Man of God my wife spoke to?"

The Angel of the Lord said to Manoah "**I AM**."

Manoah tried to offer the killing of a goat and invited the Angel of the Lord to dine with them. But the Angel of the Lord said:

> *"Though you detain Me, I will not eat your food. But if you offer a burnt offering, you must offer it to the LORD." (Judges 13:16)*

Manoah did not know He was the Angel of the LORD, so he asked the "Man of God" what His name was. To which the Angel of the Lord replied:

> *"Why do you ask My name, seeing it is wonderful?" (Judges 13:18)*

The Angel of the Lord (Christ) was about to demonstrate to Manoah through a manifestation of Holy Fire, what happens when an acceptable and pleasing sacrifice is offered unto God!

No regular Angel sent from God could make the claims this Angel made, or ever do what this Angel (Christ) did!

Why do you ask my name?

The angel of the LORD replied. It is too wonderful for you to understand!

Judges 13:18

I AM is at the doors

Manoah prepared a young goat for sacrifice and laid it on a rock before the Angel of the Lord. As the flame from the sacrifice went up towards Heaven from the altar, the Angel of the Lord ascended right into the flame on the altar! Manoah and his wife fell on their faces to the ground. They knew they had encountered God! The Lord stepped into the fire of an acceptable sacrifice!

> "And Manoah said to his wife, "We shall surely die because we have seen God!" But his wife said to him, "If the LORD had desired to kill us, He would not have accepted a burnt offering and a grain offering from our hands, nor would He have shown us all these things, nor would He have told us such things as these at this time."
> (Judges 13:22,23)

The woman bore a son and called his name Samson, which means "like the sun." As the child grew, the Lord blessed him.

In the time of the Judges, Israel was continually attacked by one of their greatest foes; the Midianites. Living in fear and trepidation, the Israelites made their homes in dens, caves, and strongholds in the mountains.

The ruthless Midianites would repeatedly come and destroy all their produce, leaving no sustenance for Israel, not even sheep, nor ox, or cattle. The Israelites were greatly impoverished because of this.

The Angel of the Lord (Christ) appeared to Gideon, who was threshing wheat inside of a winepress (to hide it from the Midianites). Gideon was surprised when the Angel said to him:

> *"The LORD is with you, you mighty man of valor!"*
> *(Judges 6:12)*

Gideon complained to the Angel of the Lord saying if the Lord was truly with us, why were they under such oppression, and not being delivered through the miracle-working hand of God?

The Angel of the Lord tells Gideon that he will be used to help save Israel and that He (the Angel) was the One sending him! Gideon then tried to convince the Angel that he was the least likely to accomplish this task since his family was the weakest tribe in Manasseh and he was the least in his father's house.

The Angel of the Lord replied:

> *"Surely I will be with you, and you shall defeat*
> *the Midianites as one man." (Judges 6:16)*

Gideon wanted to know for sure that he had favor in the sight of God, so he asked the Lord to show him a sign that it was the Lord God who was speaking to him. He asked the Angel of the

Lord to remain there until he could return to offer up a sacrifice to Him.

Gideon went and prepared a young goat and some unleavened bread. The meat he put in a basket, and the broth he put in a pot. He brought these offerings back to where he had met the Angel of the Lord.

The Lord said to Gideon:

> *"Take the meat and the unleavened bread and lay them*
> *on this rock, and pour out the broth." (Judges 6:20)*

Then an amazing thing happened! The Angel of the Lord extended out the staff that was in His hand and touched the meat and the unleavened bread, and *fire* immediately rose out of the rock and *consumed* the meat and the unleavened bread!

Gideon was undone! He now knew the Angel of the Lord he was encountering was truly God (Christ)! Gideon declared:

> *"Alas, O Lord GOD! For I have seen the **Angel of the LORD***
> *face to face." Then the LORD said to him, "Peace be with you;*
> *do not fear; you shall not die." Gideon built an altar there to*
> *the LORD, and called it The-LORD-Is-Peace. To this day, it is*
> *still in Ophrah of the Abiezrites." (Judges 6:22-24)*

As the Lord continued to manifest Himself unto man throughout the Old Testament, He most often revealed His Glorious Presence with Holy Fire!

God continually answered man with His Holy Fire, and now man was also learning to respond back to God with fire, whether being from a burned offering on the altar of sacrifice or a fire burning upon the altar of incense in prayer and intercession. We too are well on our way to understanding the Holy Fire of God! Let's continue our study!

GIDEON'S ALTAR OF FIRE

CHAPTER FIVE
THE FIRE OF ELIJAH

Chapter Five
The Fire Of Elijah

Elijah lived during a time of great idolatry in Israel. The nation was under the rule of a wicked king named Ahab and his even more wicked queen named Jezebel.

Israel was far away from God. Their hearts had turned to other gods. The most prominent of these idols in the land was one by the name of Baal.

The name Baal means "Lord." Baal was a fertility god, whom Israel looked to as their provider for crops and produce. They believed their abundance came from him. They also believed it was Baal that defeated their enemies. His image was accompanied by a lightning bolt in his right hand. Israel believed he had more power than all other gods – including Yahweh.

The women believed Baal was the one who made them fertile to have children. Baal worship was rooted in sensuality and often involved ritualistic prostitution in the temples.

Baal worship also required human sacrifice, usually with the offering of their firstborn:

> *"...they have also built the high places of Baal, to burn their sons with fire for burnt offerings to Baal..." (Jeremiah 19:5)*

The priests and prophets of Baal appealed to their god in rites of wild abandon, including loud, ecstatic cries and self-inflicted injury (cutting themselves). He was considered the "ruler of demons." He is also known as Beelzebub. (Baal-ze-bub)

71

Even Jezebel herself served under this demonic principality. Her name is Jeze-baal – meaning "Baal is husband to..." Her Father was a priest of Baal whose name was Ethbaal, which means "living with Baal, enjoying the favor and help of Baal."

Ahab, on the other hand, was the son of King Omri, the most wicked king ever seen in is Israel since the days of Jeroboam. The Bible says that King Ahab was even more wicked than his father, King Omri. What a nice couple Ahab and Jezebel made!

"Omri did evil in the eyes of the LORD and did worse than all who were before him. For he walked in all the ways of Jeroboam the son of Nebat, and in his sin by which he had made Israel sin, provoking the LORD God of Israel to anger with their idols." (1Kings 16:25, 26)

"Now Ahab the son of Omri did evil in the sight of the LORD, more than all who were before him. And it came to pass, as though it had been a trivial thing for him to walk in the sins of Jeroboam the son of Nebat that he took as wife Jezebel the daughter of Ethbaal, king of the Sidonians; and he went and served Baal and worshiped him. Then he set up an altar for Baal in the temple of Baal, which he had built in Samaria. And Ahab made a wooden image. Ahab did more to provoke the LORD God of Israel to anger than all the kings of Israel who were before him." (1 Kings 16:30-33)

God spoke to His prophet Elijah and commissioned him to go and prophesy to King Ahab concerning what the Lord was about to do in the land. Elijah declared to King Ahab there was going to be a severe drought and that Israel will stay dry except at his very decree.

"And Elijah the Tishbite, of the inhabitants of Gilead, said to Ahab,
"As the LORD God of Israel lives before whom I stand, there shall
not be dew nor rain these years, except at my word." (1 Kings 17:1)

Elijah delivered a powerful prophetic declaration, right at one the seats of power of the principality of Baal! Israel believed Baal was the provider of rain for their crops and agriculture – but now God sends a prophet to announce to King Ahab (and also to Baal) that <u>He</u> is the supreme God who "reigns" (no pun intended) over all the earth. This confrontation had all the makings for a powerful showdown as to who really was God!

About three years go by with no rain when the Lord instructs Elijah to go and present himself before King Ahab because the Lord was about to release rain upon them. But God is about to do something incredible before the entire nation!

When King Ahab and Elijah met, Ahab had the audacity to call Elijah "the troubler of Israel." Elijah confronted King Ahab and set God's plan into place.

"And he answered, "I have not troubled Israel, but you and
your father's house have, in that you have forsaken the
commandments of the LORD and have followed the Baals.
Now therefore, send and gather all Israel to me on Mount Carmel,
the four hundred and fifty prophets of Baal, and the four hundred
prophets of Asherah, who eat at Jezebel's table." (1 Kings 18:18, 19)

The children of Israel and the prophets of Baal were all gathered up on Mt. Carmel. The prophet Elijah then delivers a powerful indictment against all the peoples. He declares that they can no longer "falter" between two different opinions concerning their worship of Baal and Yahweh. He challenges them to make a choice once and for all, and to choose one or the other as their God – based on which Deity could demonstrate Himself to be the one true God!

The method God chose in proving who was the true Deity was quite amazing – because the confirmation would come in Holy Fire! Let's look in on the story from the Bible:

> *"Then Elijah said to the people, "I alone am left a prophet of the LORD; but Baal's prophets are four hundred and fifty men. Therefore let them give us two bulls, and let them choose one bull for themselves, cut it in pieces, and lay it on the wood, but put no fire under it; and I will prepare the other bull, and lay it on the wood, but put no fire under it. Then you call on the name of your gods, and I will call on the name of the LORD; and the God who <u>answers by fire</u>, **<u>He is God</u>**." So all the people answered and said, "It is well spoken." (1 Kings 18:22-24)*

The prophets of Baal took a bull and prepared it and called upon the name of Baal all morning, pleading "Oh Baal, hear us!" But nothing happened. There was no response from Baal.

By noon time, the prophet Elijah begin to drive home the point during this demonstration as to who the real God of Israel was! He mocked the prophets of Baal by saying:

> *"…Cry aloud, for he is a god; either he is meditating, or he is busy, or he is on a journey, or perhaps he is sleeping and must be awakened." So they cried aloud, and cut themselves, as was their custom, with knives and lances, until the blood gushed out on them. And when midday was past, they prophesied until the time of the offering of the evening sacrifice. But there was no voice; no one answered, no one paid attention.*
> *(1 Kings 18:27-29)*

Near evening now, it was becoming clear there would be no manifestation of power coming forth, from Baal. So Elijah called the people closer and repaired the altar of the Lord before their eyes. He placed 12 stones, representing the 12 tribes of Israel as a foundation to the altar, then cut wood and placed it on top of the rocks. Elijah then placed a cut bull's parts on top of that.

To make certain everybody knew there was no way *other* than God to come in Holy Fire to consummate the sacrifice, Elijah ordered four water pots to be filled and then poured over the sacrifice. When that was complete, he ordered four more water pots to be filled and then be poured out upon the sacrifice to soak the wood. He even did the same thing a third time, which filled up even the trenches around the sacrifice with water!

> *"And it came to pass, at the time of the offering of the evening sacrifice that Elijah the prophet came near and said, "LORD God of Abraham, Isaac, and Israel, let it be known this day that You are God in Israel and I am Your servant, and that I have done all these things at Your word. Hear me, O LORD, hear me, that this people may know that You are the LORD God, and that You have turned their hearts back to You again."*
>
> <u>*Then the fire of the LORD fell and consumed the burnt sacrifice,*</u> *and the wood and the stones and the dust, and it licked up the water that was in the trench. Now when all the people saw it, they fell on their faces; and they said,* **"The LORD, He is God! The LORD, He is God!"** *(1 Kings 18:36-39)*

The Lord first manifested Himself as a Holy Fire before Abram on Mt. Hermon, passing through the cut animals as a fiery torch. Then God came as a Holy Fire, appearing to Moses and the children of Israel, covering Mt. Sinai in the fire of His Glory!

Now the Lord comes again and demonstrates to Elijah and all of Israel on Mt. Carmel - that He *alone* is the true God – and He validates it by coming down in fiery Presence and consuming the completely drenched sacrifice! Holy Fire on the mountains!

HE IS THE GOD THAT ANSWERS BY FIRE!!!

More Fire From The God Of Elijah

After the death of Ahab, King Ahaziah ruled in the land. He fell from a second story lattice, suffering a severe injury. Wanting to know if he would live or die, he sent a delegation out to go and inquire of the God Baal about his survival.

The Angel of the Lord then told Elijah to go and confront the messengers from the king and say:

> *"Arise, go up to meet the messengers of the king of Samaria, and say to them, 'Is it because there is no God in Israel that you are going to inquire of Baal-Zebub, the god of Ekron?' Now therefore, thus says the LORD: 'You shall not come down from the bed to which you have gone up, but you shall surely die.'"*
> *(2 Kings 1:3, 4)*

The delegation went back and told King Ahaziah of their encounter and about the prophecy that he would die upon his bed. The king asked them for a description of this man and quickly realized it was Elijah the Tishbite.

The king ordered a captain with 50 men to go and capture Elijah. They found him up on a hill and declared to him the king was summoning him.

> *"So Elijah answered and said to the captain of fifty, "If I am a man of God, then let fire come down from heaven and consume you and your fifty men." And fire came down from heaven and consumed him and his fifty." (2 Kings 1:10)*

Then fire suddenly came down out of heaven and *consumed* the 50 men! Ahaziah, a stubborn king, then sent another army captain with 50 men to try and capture Elijah.

They too were met with the same results! Elijah prophesied that fire would come down from heaven and consume these 50 men... and it did!

King Ahaziah sent a third army captain with 50 men to go and arrest Elijah; only this contingency had much more respect (fear) for the Man of God than the previous two companies of soldiers. When they came to Elijah, the captain said:

> *"Man of God, please let my life and the life of these fifty servants of yours be precious in your sight. Look, fire has come down from heaven and burned up the first two captains of fifties with their fifties. But let my life now be precious in your sight."*
> *(2 Kings 1:13, 14)*

The Angel of the Lord instructed Elijah to go with them to see the king. As Elijah stood before King Ahaziah, he prophesied the king would die in his bed because of his trusting and inquiry of Baal rather than the Lord God of Israel. The king died, just as Elijah prophesied.

Elijah was with Elisha down at Gilgal when Elijah told Elisha he was going to Bethel, and for Elisha to stay there but he refused saying:

> *"As the LORD lives, and as your soul lives, I will not leave you!"* *(2 Kings 2:2)*

At Bethel, a company of prophets came out to Elisha and prophesied to him that Elijah would be taken by God that very day. Elisha confirmed to them that he knew it too.

Again, Elijah said he was leaving and going down to Jericho this time, and for Elisha to stay there, but Elisha refused, insisting he would not leave Elijah. When they got to Jericho, another company of prophets came out to meet Elisha and prophesied that God would take Elijah away that day.

Elijah then told Elisha he was going down to the Jordan, and for Elisha to stay there, and for the third time, Elisha refused to leave Elijah. Near the Jordan, Elijah took his mantle, rolled it up and struck the ground, causing the waters to part, and they both crossed over on dry ground!

Elijah asked Elisha what he may want before he was to be taken away, and Elisha requested to receive a "double-portion" of Elijah's spirit.

Suddenly a chariot of fire appeared, driven by horses of fire that came right between the two prophets, and Elijah was lifted in a whirlwind, and ascended to Heaven in a blaze of fire!

ELIJAH'S CHARIOT OF FIRE

79

CHAPTER SIX
THE FIRE OF DAVID

Chapter Six
The Fire of David

After the death of King Saul, David came out of the cave of Adullum and reigned in Hebron, over the tribe of Judah, but not over the all the rest of the other tribes.

For at that time there were two kingdoms; Judah and Israel (which was also called the Northern Kingdom), which consisted of the eleven other tribes – apart from Judah. Those tribes had remained loyal to the House of Saul, even long after King Saul's death.

Eventually, though, the leaders from the Northern Kingdom came to Hebron and were reconciled with David, thus uniting all of Israel once more, and David became King over all of Israel. Thus this fulfilled the kingly prophecy by the Prophet Samuel over David's life which he had received as a young boy.

One of the first things David did as King of Israel, was to go and attack the Jebusites and capture the stronghold of Zion! He built a city there and named the area "The City of David!"

Then King David began to raise up a mighty army. They went out and conquered surrounding nations. The Lord was with Israel, and there was great favor upon King David. His fame spread throughout all the lands, and the Lord caused the surrounding nations to fear him greatly!

David longed to see the entire nation of Israel restored to the worship of God. He decided to bring the long-neglected Ark of God to his new capital city as a sign that the Lord, the true King of Israel, was once again dwelling in the midst of His people.

David planned an elaborate procession to bring the Ark of God's Presence into Jerusalem. His plan was to involve all of Israel in that procession.

> *"Then David consulted with the captains of thousands and hundreds, and with every leader. And David said to all the assembly of Israel, "If it seems good to you, and if it is of the LORD our God, let us send out to our brethren everywhere who are left in all the land of Israel, and with them to the priests and Levites who are in their cities and their common-lands, that they may gather together to us, and let us bring the ark of our God back to us, for we have not inquired at it since the days of Saul." Then all the assembly said that they would do so, for the thing was right in the eyes of all the people." (1 Chronicles 13:1-4)*

Now the Ark had been in Shiloh for over 400 years. Shiloh had been the center of worship all those years, and all of Israel came to Shiloh three times a year to celebrate the feasts there.

At the end of the 400 years, the Israelites were fighting a heavy battle with the Philistines, and about 4,000 men in the army of Israel had been killed. After hearing the news, the elders of Israel determined their defeat was because the Ark had not been there with them – out on the battlefield, so they sent for the Ark to be brought out to the battlefield to gain their victory.

Who helps bring the Ark to the battlefield? None other than Hophni and Phinehas! They were the corrupted sons of Eli, the High Priest and had his sons had become the officiating priests of the sanctuary at Shiloh because of Eli's advancing age.

They were defiled priests, who engaged in sacrilege by having illicit sex with women who served around the sanctuary and appropriated the best portions of sacrifices for themselves.

So now we have the defiled priesthood bringing the Holy Ark of God down to the battlefield. A move that the elders of Israel did *presumptuously*, for they had not inquired of the Lord first, but did what they thought was right in their own eyes. This situation had all the makings of a major disaster!

And disaster it was! Although the Philistines were greatly troubled when they heard the cries of jubilation coming from the camp of Israel as the Ark was brought there, they decided to continue in battle. Israel suffered the loss of 30,000-foot soldiers that day. Hophni and Phinehas were also slain on the battlefield that day! But far more grievous than that, the Ark of God's Presence was captured by the Philistines!

When reports of the tragedy reached Shiloh, there was great mourning. When Eli heard the news, he fell backward and broke his neck and died. Phinehas's wife was due to give birth at that moment, and when the child was born, she named him *Ichabod*, which means "The Glory has departed."

But having possession of the Holy Ark of God proved very troubling to the Philistines. They first took the Ark to Ashdod and set it up in the temple of their god who was called Dagon. The next morning, they discovered their god had fallen during the night – right before the Ark of the Lord! They set Dagon back up, and the next morning not only was Dagon fallen again but this time both the head and the hands of Dagon were broken off as the fallen idol laid before the Ark!

The hand of the Lord was heavy upon the Philistines at Ashdod and throughout the entire territory. They were being struck with massive tumors. They knew they had to get rid of the Ark, so they took it to Gath. But the fierceness of the Lord struck that city too with great destruction, and the people with afflicted there with many tumors as well.

The Philistines learned rather quickly that trying to possess the Holy Ark of God was not such a good idea. They were frightened and wanted to lift this curse off themselves, for it became a dreadful thing to fall into the hands of the *living* God!

They brought the Ark to Ekron, where the people were in such panic, their cry went up to Heaven for the Ark to be removed!

> *"...saying, they have brought the ark of the God of Israel to us,*
> *to kill us and our people!'" So they sent and gathered together*
> *all the lords of the Philistines, and said, "Send away the ark of the*
> *God of Israel, and let it go back to its own place, so that it does not*
> *kill us and our people." For there was a deadly destruction*
> *throughout all the city; the hand of God was very heavy there.*
> *And the men who did not die were stricken with the tumors, and*
> *the cry of the city went up to heaven." (1 Samuel 5:10-12)*

The Philistines were now so terrified of the God of Israel; they conspired to return the Ark of the Lord. They recounted the terror of the Lord in Egypt against Pharaoh, and decided to add articles of gold in a chest as a trespass offering – in their attempt to try and appease God concerning the return of the Ark, hoping that no additional plagues would come upon them!

So, *they made a cart,* driven by two cows which had never been yoked before; then they placed the Ark and the chest of gold upon it. They guided it down the road towards Beth Shemesh, and there they let it go, hoping the cows would continue carrying the Ark towards the people in that city.

When the people of Beth Shemesh saw the Ark, they greatly rejoiced! They offered the two cows to the Lord as a burnt offering. But these people also made a grave mistake in that they too handled the Holy Ark of God *presumptuously*!

The Lord struck the men at Beth Shemesh that day because they had tried to look inside the Ark, and 50,070 men were killed! The people of Beth Shemesh greatly lamented because the Lord Himself had struck them with such a great slaughter.

They called forth the men of Kirjath Jearim to come and get the Ark. These men brought the Ark to the house of Abinidad on the hill and consecrated Eleazar his son to keep the Ark of the Lord, and the Ark remained there for 20 years.

David gathered all of Israel together and went to Kirjath Jearim to bring up the Ark of the Lord from there to Jerusalem.

They too put the Ark *on a cart*, which was driven by Uzzah and Ahio. Then David and all of Israel played music before the Lord with all their might, with singing, on harps, on stringed instruments, on tambourines, on cymbals, and on trumpets. You would think the Lord would greatly pleased… right?

But when they reached Chidon's threshing floor, Uzzah put out his hand to steady the Ark, for the oxen had stumbled. Suddenly the anger of the Lord was aroused against Uzzah, and the Lord struck him, and he died right there before God and all of Israel!

The anger of the Lord was aroused not only at Uzzah by touching the Ark, but also towards David, his leaders, and the priests. They had completely disregarded the instruction of the Lord, and the ordinances God had given previously to Moses and Aaron concerning the handling, and the moving of the Ark… none of which they properlyco0nsidered or regarded when they made plans to move the Ark to Jerusalem.

David was now afraid to move the Ark any further, so they took the Ark to the house of Obed-Edom, a Levite. The Ark remained at the home of Obed-Edom for three months.

The Lord had given clear instructions about the handling and moving of the Ark in the Word of God (Torah). It was *only* to be performed by the sons (descendants) of Kohath.

> *"And when Aaron and his sons have finished covering the sanctuary and all the furnishings of the sanctuary, when the camp is set to go, then the sons of Kohath shall come to carry them; but they shall not touch any holy thing, lest they die. These are the things in the tabernacle of meeting which the sons of Kohath are to carry." (Numbers 4:15)*

No matter how innocently it was done, touching the Ark was in direct violation of God's law and was to result in death. This was a means of preserving the sense of God's Holiness and the fear of drawing near to Him without appropriate preparation.

Not only had David violated the ordinance of God in the moving of the Ark, but he also allowed the people to put the Ark *on a cart* (like the Philistines had). The Ark was never meant to be moved on a *man–made* cart, but only upon the shoulders of the Levites (Priesthood). They didn't even use the poles specifically designed by God to insert into the rings on the side of the Ark in which in which to carry it!

> *"You shall cast four rings of gold for it and put them on its four feet, two rings on the one side of it, and two rings on the other side of it. You shall make poles of acacia wood and overlay them with gold. And you shall put the poles into the rings on the sides of the ark to carry the ark by them." (Exodus 25:12-14)*

David prepared a place for the Holy Ark of God in the City of David, having pitched a tent for it. This time around, David followed the Divine protocol of God for moving the Ark:

> *"Then David said, "No one may carry the ark of God <u>but the Levites, for the LORD has chosen them to carry the ark of God and to minister before Him forever</u>." And David gathered all Israel together at Jerusalem, to bring up the ark of the LORD to its place, which he had prepared for it. Then David assembled the children of Aaron and the Levites: of* **the sons of Kohath**, *Uriel the chief, and one hundred and twenty of his brethren; of the sons of Merari, Asaiah the chief, and two hundred and twenty of his brethren; of the sons of Gershom, Joel the chief, and one hundred and thirty of his brethren; of the sons of Elizaphan, Shemaiah the chief, and two hundred of his brethren; of the sons of Hebron, Eliel the chief, and eighty of his brethren; of the sons of Uzziel, Amminadab the chief, and one hundred and twelve of his brethren." (1 Chronicles 15:2-10)*

> *"And David called for Zadok and Abiathar the priests, and for the Levites: for Uriel, Asaiah, Joel, Shemaiah, Eliel, and Amminadab. He said to them, "You are the heads of the fathers' houses of the Levites; sanctify yourselves, you and your brethren, that you may bring up the Ark of the LORD God of Israel to the place I have prepared for it... For*

*because you did not do it the first time, the LORD our God broke out against us, **because we did not consult Him about the proper order**."*

So the priests and the Levites sanctified themselves to bring up the ark, and bore the ark of God on their shoulders, by its poles, as Moses had commanded according to the word of the LORD." (1 Chronicles 15:11-15)

What a jubilant procession that must have been! David appointed singers, dancers, musicians, psalmists and all of Israel to march forth in high praise as the Ark was transported to the City of David in Jerusalem.

There was great shouting, trumpets blaring, and open worship being lifted up to the God of Israel! David was dancing and whirling around, and playing music *with all his might*!

They placed the Ark in the Tabernacle of David, and David appointed Asaph and other singers and musicians to minister praise unto God continually before the Ark of His Presence.

Not long after these incredible mistakes (and achievements) in the life of King David, Satan came and moved upon David to number Israel, and so a census was decreed among the people. Joab was put in charge of the census, but even he had great reservations about doing such a thing:

"And Joab answered, "May the LORD make His people a hundred times more than they are. But, my lord the king, are they not all my lord's servants? Why then does my lord require this thing? Why should he be a cause of guilt in Israel?"
(1 Chronicles 21:3)

90

Nevertheless, Joab conducted the census and reported back to David the count – (except for the tribes of Levi and Benjamin).

> *"But he did not count Levi and Benjamin among them, for the king's word was abominable to Joab."* (1 Chronicles 21:6)

God was so displeased with this act that He struck Israel. David soon realized that he had sinned greatly before the Lord in this matter and cried out to God:

> *"So David said to God, "I have sinned greatly, because I have done this thing; but now, I pray, take away the iniquity of Your servant, for I have done very foolishly."* (1 Chronicles 21:8)

The Lord moved upon Gad, who was a seer for David, and instructed him to go to David and tell him:

> *"…Thus says the LORD: "I offer you three things; choose one of them for yourself, that I may do it to you. So Gad came to David and said to him, "Thus says the LORD: 'Choose for yourself, either three years of famine, or three months to be defeated by your foes with the sword of your enemies overtaking you, or else for three days the sword of the LORD—the plague in the land, with the angel of the LORD destroying throughout all the territory of Israel.' Now consider what answer I should take back to Him who sent me."* (1 Chronicles 21:912)

David was deeply distraught by such a judgment. He pleaded with God that he might fall into the hand of the Lord and His great mercies… but not into the hands of man!

But the Lord sent a plague upon Israel, and 70,000 men died. God had sent an angel to destroy Jerusalem, but as the angel was destroying the city, the Lord looked and relented of the disaster and restrained that angel from further damage.

Then suddenly **the Angel of the Lord** (Christ) stood at the threshing floor of Ornan, the Jebusite.

David lifted his eyes and saw the Angel of the Lord (Christ) standing between earth and heaven, with a sword drawn out across Jerusalem. David and the elders, clothed in sackcloth, fell on their faces, and David then said *the Angel of the Lord:*

> *"Was it not I who commanded the people to be numbered? I am the one who has sinned and done evil indeed; but these sheep, what have they done? Let Your hand, I pray, O LORD my God, be against me and my father's house, but not against Your people that they should be plagued." (1 Chronicles 21:17)*

The Angel of the Lord commanded Gad to tell David to build an altar to the Lord upon the very threshing floor of Ornan, so David went and pleaded with Ornan to sell him the threshing floor there so he could build an altar to God on it.

Ornan tried to offer it to David for free, but David insisted on paying full price for it.

> *"Then King David said to Ornan, "No, but I will surely buy it for the full price, for I will not take what is yours for the LORD, nor offer burnt offerings with that which costs me nothing." So David gave Ornan six hundred shekels of gold by weight for the place." (1 Chronicles 21:24, 25)*

So, David built an altar there to the Lord, where he offered up burnt offerings and peace offerings. The sacrifice was acceptable and pleasing to the Lord, after such a tumultuous set of events in the life of David and Israel.

The Bible says that the Lord *answered* David's offerings by **Holy Fire** coming down out of Heaven and completely consuming David's sacrifice!

The Fire of Heaven was burning on the altar of David!

That very altar would later become the exact location site for the building of the first Temple by David's son Solomon. The location of David's altar of Holy Fire took place on Ornan's threshing floor which was located on a mountain range called the Mountains of Mt. Moriah, on a hill called Zion.

KING DAVID'S ALTAR OF FIRE AT THE THRESHING FLOOR OF ORNAN

CHAPTER SEVEN
THE FIRE OF
SOLOMON

Chapter Seven
The Fire of Solomon

King David dwelled in a beautiful and glorious palace of choice cedar, built for him by King Hiram of Tyre. Life was good for David, for he has reconciled the two kingdoms of Israel, captured the stronghold of Zion, and made Jerusalem his Capital. He had also brought the Ark of the Covenant to Jerusalem and made it the center of religious worship.

The Lord had given David both blessed rest and peace from all his enemies:

> *"King David was living in his palace, and the LORD had given*
> *him peace from all his enemies around him." (2 Chronicles 7:1)*

It gave King David time to ponder and reflect. As he did, he came to a conclusion, *"Here I am, living in a house of cedar, while the Ark of God remains in a tent."* He then gets the dream to build God a glorious Temple – a home for the Ark of the Covenant that would replace the Tabernacle tent.

So David calls upon Nathan, the Prophet and shares his idea with Nathan, who also thinks it's a good idea. But Nathan goes home that night and receives a "Word" from the Lord...

> *"Go and tell my servant David, 'This is what the LORD says:*
> *Will you build a house for me to live in? From the time I*
> *brought the Israelites out of Egypt until now I have not lived in a*
> *house. I have been moving around all this time with a tent as*
> *my home. As I have moved with the Israelites, I have never said*
> *to the tribes, whom I commanded to take care of my people Israel,*
> *"Why haven't you built me a house of cedar?"' (2 Chronicles 7:5-7)*

Apparently, God did not think it was as good of an idea as David did. The Lord reiterated this several times throughout the whole of Scripture:

> *"Heaven is My throne, and earth is My footstool.*
> *Where is the house that you will build Me? And where*
> *is the place of My rest? For all those things My hand*
> *has made, and all those things exist," Says the LORD.*
> *"But on this one will I look: on him who is poor and of*
> *a contrite spirit, and who trembles at My word."*
> *(Isaiah 66:1, 2)*

> *"God, who made the world and everything in it, since*
> *He is Lord of heaven and earth, does not dwell in temples*
> *made with hands. Nor is He worshiped with men's hands,*
> *as though He needed anything, since He gives to all life,*
> *breath, and all things." (Acts 17:24, 25)*

Though David's plan was to build God a Temple, God's plan was to build *David*!

> *"…This is what the LORD All-Powerful says: I took you from*
> *the pasture and from tending the sheep and made you leader*
> *of my people Israel. I have been with you everywhere you have*
> *gone and have defeated your enemies for you. I will make you*
> *as famous as any of the great people on the earth. Also I will*
> *choose a place for my people Israel, and I will plant them so*
> *they can live in their own homes. They will not be bothered*
> *anymore. Wicked people will no longer bother them as they*
> *have in the past when I chose judges for my people Israel. But*
> *I will give you peace from all your enemies. I also tell you*
> *that I will make your descendants kings of Israel after you."*
> *(2 Chronicles 7:8-11)*

Then God reveals to David *"You want to build Me a house? I am going to build you a house – and not just any house!"* God lets

David know He is going to honor David's dream and build a Temple that bears His name, but that He will build it through his son Solomon, because David had been a man of war with bloodshed on his hands, but his son Solomon was a man of peace.

But then God reveals far more to David! The Lord tells him that upon his throne, the Most High God will build an everlasting Throne that will never end. God is revealing to David that from the succession of his throne there will come, Christ the Eternal King, who will sit on the throne of David forever!

> *"...Furthermore I tell you **that the LORD will build you a house**.*
> *And it shall be, when your days are fulfilled, when you must go*
> *to be with your fathers, that I will set up your seed after you,*
> *who will be of your sons; and I will establish his kingdom. He*
> *shall build Me a house, and I will establish his throne forever.*
> *I will be his Father, and he shall be My son; and I will not take*
> *My mercy away from him, as I took it from him who was before*
> *you. And I will establish him in My house and in My kingdom*
> *forever; and his throne shall be established forever."*
> *(1 Chronicles 17:10-14)*

> *"The LORD has sworn in truth to David; He will not turn from*
> *it: "I will set upon your throne the fruit of your body." (Psalm 132:11)*

> *"I have made a covenant with My chosen, I have sworn to My*
> *servant David: 'Your seed I will establish forever, and build*
> *up your throne to all generations." Selah (Psalm 89:3, 4)*

> *"...let me speak freely to you of the patriarch David... Therefore,*
> *being a prophet, and knowing that God had sworn with an oath*
> *to him that of the fruit of his body, according to the flesh, He would*
> *raise up the Christ to sit on his throne..." (Acts 2:29-31*

David had laid up a vast supply of treasure in gold, silver, brass, and iron in anticipation for the building of the Temple. He gave these precious materials to his son Solomon for the construction of the Temple, but that wasn't all David gave him:

*"Then David gave his son Solomon the **plans** for the vestibule, its houses, its treasuries, its upper chambers, its inner chambers, and the place of the mercy seat; **and the plans for all that he had by the Spirit**, of the courts of the house of the LORD, of all the chambers all around, of the treasuries of the house of God, and of the treasuries for the dedicated things; also for the division of the priests and the Levites, for all the work of the service of the house of the LORD, and for all the articles of service in the house of the LORD.*

*He gave gold by weight for things of gold, for all articles used in every kind of service; also silver for all articles of silver by weight, for all articles used in every kind of service; the weight for the lampstands of gold, and their lamps of gold, by weight for each lampstand and its lamps; for the lampstands of silver by weight, for the lampstand and its lamps, according to the use of each lampstand. And by weight he gave gold for the tables of the showbread, for each table, and silver for the tables of silver; also pure gold for the forks, the basins, the pitchers of pure gold, and the golden bowls — he gave gold by weight for every bowl; and for the silver bowls, silver by weight for every bowl; and refined gold by weight for the altar of incense, and for the construction of the chariot, that is, the gold cherubim that spread their wings and overshadowed the ark of the covenant of the LORD. 'All this' said David, **"the LORD made me understand in writing, by His hand upon me, all the works of these plans**." (1 Chronicles 28:11-19)*

The revelation of the plans for building the Temple had been given to David by the Holy Spirit, which he then handed down to his son Solomon. The building of this Temple became the crowning achievement of Solomon's reign as King of Israel.

Solomon took all that he had received from his father David and began to build. He conferred with King Hiram of Tyre and arranged for massive amounts of beautiful, fragrant cedar lumber to be shipped in from the region of Lebanon, with gold, and other materials, but Solomon went deep into debt doing this and had to pay King Hiram with 20 cities up in the Galilee.

"King Solomon gave twenty towns in Galilee to Hiram king of Tyre, because Hiram had supplied him with all the cedar and juniper and gold he wanted." (1 Kings 9:11)

Solomon gathered 30,000 laborers to assist in bringing the materials back from King Hiram. He sent them to Lebanon in work shifts of 10,000 at a time for one month, so they would spend one month at work and then two months home.

At home, Solomon had 70,000 laborers (carriers), and 80,000 stonecutters. These artisan craftsmen cut out marble stone in the hills and local quarries, and pre-cut the stone with precision before bringing the pieces up to the Temple building site. It was a marvel that the construction of the Temple was built in near silence.

"When the house was built, it was with stone prepared at the quarry, so that neither hammer nor ax nor any tool of iron was heard in the house while it was being built." (1 Kings 6:7)

Inside the Temple, skilled woodworkers had carved out ornate, beautiful buds, cherubim's, palm trees and open flowers upon the wood panels throughout the Temple. Then the entire inside of the Temple was completely overlaid with gold!

Solomon set 3300 foremen over the project to supervise the operation. It was an incredible feat – but the most glorious Temple on earth was finally built! It took seven years to finish.

Once the Temple was complete, Solomon assembled the elders of Israel, the heads of all the tribes, and the chief fathers of the children of Israel. Along with the priests and the Levites, they went into the City of David, which is Zion and brought the Ark of the Covenant into its new home in the inner sanctuary the Temple – called the Holy of Holies.

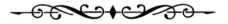

The priests came out of the Holy Place, after having sanctified themselves. The Levitical singers, Asaph, Heman, and Jeduthun appeared, along with their sons and kindred, all arrayed in fine linen, with cymbals, harps, and lyres and they stood east of the altar with one hundred and twenty priests who were trumpeters.

It was the duty of the trumpeters and singers to make themselves heard in unison of praise and thanksgiving to the Lord. They lifted up a song, with trumpets and cymbals and other musical instruments, in praise to the Lord, singing: *"For He is good, and His steadfast love endures forever."*

Then an amazing thing happened! The house of the Lord was *filled* with a cloud so that the priests could not even stand to minister because of the cloud; for the Glory of the Lord filled the house of God!

Then Solomon kneeled before the altar of the Lord in the presence of the whole assembly of Israel and spread out his hands towards Heaven. Solomon then began to dedicate the Temple unto the Mighty God of Israel!

*"He said, 'O Lord, God of Israel, there is no God like You, in Heaven
or on earth, keeping covenant in steadfast love with Your servants
who walk before You with all their heart— You who have kept for
Your servant, my father David, what You promised to him. Indeed,
You promised with Your mouth and this day have fulfilled with Your
hand. Therefore, O Lord, God of Israel, keep for Your servant, my
father David, that which You promised him, saying, "There shall
never fail you a successor before Me to sit on the throne of Israel,
if only your children keep to their way, to walk in My law as you
have walked before Me." Therefore, O Lord, God of Israel, let Your
word be confirmed, which You promised to your servant David.*

*'But will God indeed reside with mortals on earth? Even heaven
and the highest Heaven cannot contain You, how much less this
house that I have built! Have regard to Your servant's prayer and
his plea, O Lord my God, heeding the cry and the prayer that Your
servant prays to You. May Your eyes be open day and night towards
this house, the place where You promised to set Your Name, and
may You heed the prayer that Your servant prays towards this place.
And hear the plea of Your servant and Your people Israel when
they pray towards this place; may You hear from Heaven, Your
dwelling-place; hear and forgive."* (2 Chronicles 6:14-21)

*"Now rise up, O Lord God, and go to Your resting place,
You and the Ark of Your Might. Let Your priests, O Lord God,
be clothed with salvation, and let Your faithful rejoice in Your
Goodness. O Lord God, do not reject Your anointed one.
Remember Your steadfast love for Your servant David."*
(2 Chronicles 6:41, 42)

When Solomon had ended his prayer, Holy Fire came down
from Heaven and consumed the burnt-offering and the
sacrifices, and the Glory of the Lord filled the Temple. The

priests could not even enter the house of the Lord because the Glory of the Lord that filled the Lord's house was so intense!

When all the people of Israel saw the Holy Fire come down and the Glory of the Lord in the Temple, they bowed down on the pavement with their faces to the ground and worshiped and gave thanks to the Lord, saying:

"For He is good, for his steadfast love endures forever."
(2 Chronicles 7:3)

THE HOLY FIRE OF GOD
AT THE DEDICATION
OF SOLOMON'S TEMPLE

CHAPTER EIGHT
THE FIRE OF EZEKIEL

Chapter Eight
The Fire Of Ezekiel

The Prophet Ezekiel, whose name means "God Strengthens" was trained in the priesthood, and most likely a member of the Zadok priestly family, which came to prominence during the reforms of King Josiah.

Ezekiel had been exiled to Babylon during the second siege of Jerusalem, and settled in Tel Abib, on the Chebar Canal.

He wrote under a heavy prophetic anointing to those who were still in Jerusalem about its imminent destruction, including the departure of God's Presence. He was a contemporary of the Prophet Jeremiah who also foretold of the destruction of Jerusalem and the exile to Babylon.

His wife died at about the same time as the destruction of Jerusalem in 587 B.C. God forbid Ezekiel to mourn for his wife as a prophetic sign and gesture to the people that they were not to mourn for Jerusalem and the fall of that city because of sin.

"Also the word of the LORD came to me, saying,"Son of man, behold, I take away from you the desire of your eyes with one stroke; yet you shall neither mourn nor weep, nor shall your tears run down. Sigh in silence, make no mourning for the dead; bind your turban on your head, and put your sandals on your feet; do not cover your lips, and do not eat man's bread of sorrow." (Ezekiel 24:16, 17)

Thus Ezekiel is a sign to you; according to all that he has done you shall do; and when this comes, you shall know that I am the Lord GOD.'" (Ezekiel 24:24)

The River Chebar is mentioned eight times in the Bible, and all eight occurrences are in the Book of Ezekiel. The Chebar Canal was thought to be the Royal Canal of King Nebuchadnezzar.

It was along the banks of this canal that the Prophet Ezekiel experienced a glorious vision – for the Spirit of the Lord had come upon Ezekiel and empowered him to see into the Heavenly realms of Glory!

But what exactly did say he saw? He said he saw a *whirlwind* coming out of the North as a great cloud of raging, Holy Fire!

> *"Then I looked, and behold, a whirlwind was coming out of the north, a great cloud with raging fire engulfing itself; and brightness was all around it and radiating out of its midst like the color of amber, out of the midst of the fire." (Ezekiel 1:4)*

Ezekiel then saw four living creatures, and each one of them had four faces and four wings. The four faces of each creature were that of a man, a lion, an ox, and an eagle. Their wings touched one another, and these creatures sparkled like the color of burnished bronze.

As for the likeness of the living creatures, their appearance was like burning coals of fire, like the appearance of torches going back and forth among the living creatures. The fire was bright, and out of the fire went forth lightning. And the living creatures ran back and forth, in appearance like a flash of lightning.

Ezekiel was witnessing an amazing sight! As he continues to behold these fiery creatures, (which Ezekiel later identifies in Chapter 10 as *"Cherubim"*), he begins to see a wheel beside each creature upon the earth. The *workings* of these cherubim were like a wheel within another wheel. The wheels had high rims (perhaps reaching from Earth to Heaven) and were full of eyes, which symbolizes God's *all-seeing* nature.

Wherever the Spirit (Ruach) wanted to go – they went too, for the wheels were lifted up with them, and the Spirit was inside the wheels. Whenever they move in any of the four directions (towards the four corners of the earth), they also moved forward, not turning to the side. The whole description seemed to symbolize the omnipresence of God – who is capable of moving in *any* direction.

Above the living creatures was a firmament (referring to the expanse of Heaven that God had created on the second Day of creation), which separated the waters above from the waters below. It was like unto the color of awesome crystal, stretched out over the heads of these living creatures.

Under the firmament, their wings spread out straight, toward one another. Each creature had two wings which covered one side of their body, and two wings which covered the other side of their body. When they moved, the noise of their wings was like the sound of many waters - like the Voice of the Almighty, like the tumult of a mighty army. Whenever the living creatures stood still, they let down their wings.

Also above the firmament over their heads was the likeness of a Throne, that in appearance looked like a sparkling sapphire stone. And then what Ezekiel witnessed there was beyond anything he had ever seen before in his entire life!

He saw the One seated upon the Throne – the very **I AM**!!

And what did the I AM, the Eternal Son of God, Christ Jesus, appear as? Ezekiel described the awesome God as clearly as he could! He said he saw Jesus, *clothed* in Holy Fire!

What Ezekiel described was the likeness of the Throne and the appearance of a Man high above it. From the appearance of this Man's waist and upward, Ezekiel saw the color of amber with <u>Holy Fire</u> wrapped all around Him, and from the waist down he also saw the appearance of fire with brightness all around Him. Like the appearance of a rainbow in a cloud on a rainy day so was the very brightness all around Him. It was the appearance of the Glory of the Lord!

When Ezekiel saw Him, he fell on his face, and then he heard the Voice of the One speaking.

> And He said to me, "Son of man, stand on your feet, and I will speak to you." Then the Spirit entered me when He spoke to me, and set me on my feet; and I heard Him who spoke to me. And He said to me: "Son of man, I am sending you to the children of Israel, to a rebellious nation that has rebelled against Me; they and their fathers have transgressed against Me to this very day. For they are impudent and stubborn children. I am sending you to them, and you shall say to them, '**Thus says <u>the Lord GOD</u>.**' As for them, whether they hear or whether they refuse—for they are a rebellious house—yet they will know that a prophet has been among them.

> "And you, son of man, do not be afraid of them nor be afraid of their words, though briers and thorns are with you and you dwell among scorpions; do not be afraid of their words or dismayed by their looks, though they are a rebellious house. You shall speak My words to them, whether they hear or whether they refuse, for they are rebellious. But you, son of man, hear what I say to you. Do not be rebellious like that rebellious house; open your mouth and eat what I give you." (Ezekiel 2:1-8)

As Ezekiel was looking upon this God, who was shimmering in Holy Fire and Glory all around Him, the Lord stretched out His hand towards Ezekiel and in His hand, was the scroll of a book. Then the Lord spread it out before Ezekiel, and he saw that there was writing on both the inside and the outside of the book. The writings were of lamentations, mourning, and woe.

Ezekiel was stunned by the whole experience, especially by seeing and hearing the Voice of the Lord (King Jesus) speaking to him, for the Lord had spoken to Ezekiel using a specific vernacular. He referred to Himself as, *"the Lord God."*

The Lord was using a compound name to refer to Himself. Translated it would be:

Lord: Adonai (Lord)

God: Jehovah (YHWH, I AM)

Ezekiel was deeply impacted by both the revelation and the commission he received from this Holy God, the One whom he saw wrapped in Holy Fire, sitting on the Throne, declaring Himself to be **"the Lord, I AM."**

The Book of Ezekiel refers to this name, **"the Lord, I AM"** an incredible 216 more times in the writings of Ezekiel! To put things in perspective – that particular name of God is only used 103 times throughout the rest of the entire Old Testament!

This name of God emphasizes Sovereignty, as it is the *personal* name of God, who made Himself known to man and entered into Covenant with His people.

The Lord then tells Ezekiel to eat the scroll He has placed in his hands. The scroll tasted like sweet *honey*. The Lord then charges Ezekiel to go to the house of Israel and prophesy, for the house of Israel had become calloused, rebellious and dull of hearing. Ezekiel's prophetic message was to prepare them for the destruction of Jerusalem and the Temple.

Ezekiel said the Spirit lifted him up, (a frequent expression of Ezekiel's to indicate the active involvement of the Spirit in the revelatory process). Then he heard a great, thunderous voice say *"Blessed the Glory of the Lord from His Place."* Then Ezekiel heard the noise of the wings of the creatures that touched one another, and the noise of the wheels beside them, and a great thunderous noise.

As the Spirit had lifted him up and carried him away, Ezekiel went in bitterness, and in the heat of his spirit; but the hand of the Lord was strong upon him. Ezekiel came to the captives at Tel Abib, who dwelt by the River Chebar; and there he sat, *astonished*, for seven days.

After seven days, the word of the Lord came to Ezekiel saying:

*"Son of man, I have made you a watchman for the house
of Israel; therefore hear a word from My mouth, and give them
warning from Me: When I say to the wicked, 'You shall surely
die,' and you give him no warning, nor speak to warn the wicked
from his wicked way, to save his life, that same wicked man shall
die in his iniquity; but his blood I will require at your hand. Yet,
if you warn the wicked, and he does not turn from his wickedness,
nor from his wicked way, he shall die in his iniquity; but you
have delivered your soul.*

Son of man, I have made you a watchman for the house of Israel;
therefore hear a word from My mouth, and give them warning
from Me: When I say to the wicked, 'You shall surely die,'
and you give him no warning, nor speak to warn the wicked from
his wicked way, to save his life, that same wicked man shall die
in his iniquity; but his blood I will require at your hand. Yet, if
you warn the wicked, and he does not turn from his wickedness,
nor from his wicked way, he shall die in his iniquity; but you
have delivered your soul. (Ezekiel 3:17-21)

The Lord places a mantle and a mandate upon Ezekiel as a prophet to the nation of Israel. The level of accountability to the Old Testament prophet is staggering. If he doesn't deliver the indictment of the Lord to the people concerning their wickedness, so that they may repent and receive new life and restored their relationship with God, that if they die in their iniquity, the Lord will charge Ezekiel, as having "their blood upon his account!"

The Lord instructed Ezekiel to go out to the plain, and when he did, again he saw the Glory of the Lord as he had at the River Chebar. There the Lord continued to prepare His chosen Prophet to go and prophesy to the rebellious house of Israel through Divine utterance and prophetic, symbolic gestures.

On one such gesture, the Lord required Ezekiel to lay on his left side as to lay the iniquity of Israel upon it. He laid there for 390 days, each day representing a year of the iniquity of Israel. If that were not bad enough, the Lord then called Ezekiel to lay on his right side for 40 more days so as to bear the number of years of the iniquity of Judah.

Ezekiel has yet another encounter with the God of Holy Fire as he was sitting in his house with the elders of Judah when the hand (Holy Spirit) of the Lord fell upon him.

"Then I looked, and there was a likeness, like the appearance of fire—from the appearance of His waist and downward, fire; and from His waist and upward, like the appearance of brightness, like the color of amber. He stretched out the form of a hand, and took me by a lock of my hair; and the Spirit lifted me up between earth and heaven, and brought me in visions of God to Jerusalem, to the door of the north gate of the inner court, where the seat of the image of jealousy was, which provokes to jealousy. And behold, the glory of the God of Israel was there, like the vision that I saw in the plain." (Ezekiel 8:2-4)*

In every experience now, Ezekiel has with God; he has encountered the Lord completely engulfed in Holy Fire. The Lord causes Ezekiel to see what God sees, the incredible wickedness, idol worship, and vile acts that the nation of Israel commits every day – both in and around the Temple!

The Lord showed Ezekiel the North entrance to the Temple with an image of the fertility goddess Asherah. Ezekiel was made to understand that this idolatrous image was the very *seat* (throne, dwelling place) of that deity which was called the "*image of jealousy.*" Portrayed all around the walls inside were other heavily demonic relief drawings (like ancient Egyptian drawings or hieroglyphics) of every kind.

"Furthermore He said to me, "Son of man, do you see what they are doing, the great abominations that the house of Israel commits here, to make Me go far away from My sanctuary? Now turn again, you will see greater abominations." (Ezekiel 8:6)

114

" So I went in and saw, and there—every sort of creeping thing,
abominable beasts, and all the idols of the house of Israel,
portrayed all around on the walls." (Ezekiel 8:10)

In another corner of the temple, there were women weeping and crying out for Tammuz, a pagan shepherd god who the Jews believed married the goddess Ishtar. When he died, they believed all fertility stopped in Israel, so these women were in travail and intercession, crying out to this vegetation deity.

In another corner of the Temple, 25 men, with their backs turned *away* from the Temple were ardently worshipping the sun in the east.

It was the most deplorable situation you could imagine! The Lord was both enraged, heartbroken and jealous. God was about to issue His Decree for judgment and summoned His warrior Angels who have charge over the city.

Six Angels came forth, and one of them had an inkhorn in his hand. The Lord commissions him to go throughout the city and put a "mark" on the foreheads of men who sigh and cry over all the abominations that are committed in Jerusalem.

"and the LORD said to him, "Go through the midst of the city,
through the midst of Jerusalem, and put a mark on the foreheads
of the men who sigh and cry over all the abominations that are
done within it." (Ezekiel 9:4)

The Hebrew word for "mark" is *taw*, which is the last letter of the Hebrew alphabet. In the ancient Hebraic script, it looked like an "X" or a cross. The mark was for protection and symbolized that God would spare the righteous remnant.

115

For the righteous of the city, it went well for them, as the Angel with the inkhorn went about the city, putting the seal of God on their foreheads. To the unrighteous, Ezekiel hears what the Lord spoke to His other Angels that have charge of the city:

> *"To the others He said in my hearing, "Go after him through the city and kill; do not let your eye spare, nor have any pity. Utterly slay old and young men, maidens and little children and women; but do not come near anyone on whom is the mark; and begin at My sanctuary." So they began with the elders who were before the temple. Then He said to them, "Defile the temple, and fill the courts with the slain. Go out!" And they went out and killed in the city." (Ezekiel 9:5-7)*

Note that the Lord had said, "<u>*Begin at My Sanctuary,*</u>" for judgment begins – at the House of God.

Then Ezekiel's vision was directed towards the Throne in Heaven again. He sees an Angel clothed in linen, who is instructed to go in among the wheels of Fire and Glory, and to fill his hands with coals of fire from among the Cherubim – to scatter over the city.

There were Cherubim at the Temple, and when the Angel went in, the Glory of the Lord filled the entire House. The sound of the wings of the Cherubim was loud – like the Voice of the Almighty when He speaks. Again an Angel is told to take fire from among the wheels, and one Cherub put the fire into the hands of another Cherub.

Then Ezekiel watched as the Glory of the Lord departed from the Temple, and the Cherubim lifted their wings and mounted up from the earth – out of Ezekiel's sight. *Ichabod!*

So once more we see the Holy Fire that surrounds our God, His Angels, as well as the wheels of the Chariot–Throne that Ezekiel saw. Holy Fire had been gathered from Heaven, from within the wheels, around the Cherubim and cast upon the city in judgment.

Remember… The Holy Fire of God can come in blessing, or it can come in judgment!

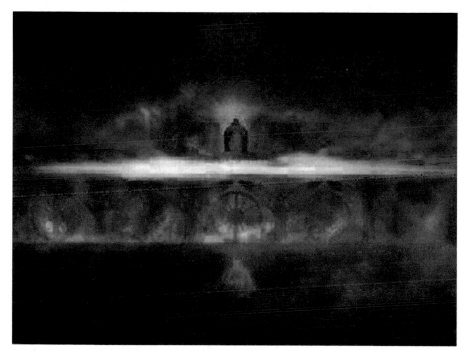

EZEKIEL'S VISION OF
THE CHARIOT–THRONE

CHAPTER NINE
SHADRACH, MESHACH & ABEDNEGO

Chapter Nine
Shadrach, Meshach & Abednego

Thousands of captives had been exiled from Judah during the siege of Jerusalem by King Nebuchadnezzar around 605 B.C. which lasted for several years. They were carried away as captives to Babylon.

At that time, the Babylonians had subdued all the provinces ruled by Assyria and had consolidated them into a vast and powerful empire that covered much of the Middle East.

To govern such a diversified kingdom over such a large geographical area required a significant amount of skilled and talented man–power. Among the first wave of Israelites taken prisoner were those from upper-class families in Jerusalem who were highly educated and known to possess both wisdom and knowledge.

Taken during the first exile were Daniel, Hananiah, Mishael, Azariah, whose skills, character and appearance landed them high–level positions in the king's palace.

King Nebuchadnezzar decided to build a massive gold idol in the plain of Dura, in the province of Babylon. This statue was 60 cubits tall and 60 cubits wide.

The king sent forth a decree to summon all of the satraps, administrators, governors, counselors, treasurers, judges, magistrates and other officials to come and attend the dedication of the idol.

As the dedication began, a herald cried out:

*"To you it is commanded, O peoples, nations, and languages, that
at the time you hear the sound of the horn, flute, harp, lyre, and
psaltery, in symphony with all kinds of music, you shall fall down
and worship the gold image that King Nebuchadnezzar has set up;
and whoever does not fall down and worship shall be cast immediately
into the midst of a burning fiery furnace." (Daniel 3:4-6)*

At that time, certain Chaldeans came forward to bring an accusation against the dispersed Jews now living in Babylon. They spoke to King Nebuchadnezzar and reminded the king of his decree that *everyone* must fall down and worship the gold image at the sound of the horn, flute, harp, lyre, and psaltery playing together like a symphony. They also reminded the king that whoever did not fall down and worship the image was to be cast into a fiery furnace.

The Chaldeans went on to specifically name Hananiah, Mishael, and Azariah, who had received the Persian names of Shadrach, Meshach, and Abednego. They declared to King Nebuchadnezzar that these three had not paid due homage regarding him, and do not serve his gods, or worship the gold image that the king had set up.

King Nebuchadnezzar was furious, and in rage, he gave the command that Shadrach, Meshach, and Abednego be brought to him. So the king asked them if it was true that they do not worship his gods and refused to bow down to his gold image when the music was played in the land.

The king reminded them that the consequences of not obeying his decree would cause them to be cast into the fiery furnace. Then the king angrily declared:

"And who is the god who will deliver you from my hands?"

Shadrach, Meshach, and Abednego responded to the king in a most powerful and resolute way. They said:

"O Nebuchadnezzar, we have no need to answer you in this matter. If that is the case, our God whom we serve is able to deliver us from the burning fiery furnace, and He will deliver us from your hand, O king. But if not, let it be known to you, O king, that we do not serve your gods, nor will we worship the gold image which you have set up." Daniel (3:16-18)

What a brilliant display of courage, for Shadrach, Meshach, and Abednego chose to remain faithful in their separation unto God, and demonstrated an uncompromising spirit in the face of such a spectacular test of faith!

Now King Nebuchadnezzar was full of fury, and the expression showed on his face. He commanded that the heat of the furnace be turned up *seven times* hotter than the normal temperature it was normally heated at.

The king then ordered certain mighty men in his army to bind Shadrach, Meshach, and Abednego and then to cast into the fiery furnace.

Because the king had commanded the heat of the furnace to be turned up *seven times*, the heat was so severely hot that as the king's mighty men were casting Shadrach, Meshach, and Abednego into the fire – the flames of the fire devoured all of the king's men, and they perished instantly!

The king thought the matter was resolved, according to his edict. He had no idea at the moment that the Holy Fire of God's Presence had come upon the scene!

The Scriptures tell us that Christ, our Lord, had stepped into the fiery furnace! The Lord came and surrounded His servants with protection, for although Shadrach, Meshach, and Abednego had been thrown into the furnace – they were not instantly cremated.

Could they have been protected with same Holy Fire that came and separated the Israelites from the Egyptians at the Red Sea crossing which acted as a barrier of protection to them also?

Could it also have been the same Holy Fire of protection that the Lord promised He would surround Jerusalem with?

> *"For I,' says the LORD, 'will be a **wall of fire** all around her,*
> *and I will be the glory in her midst." (Zechariah 2:5)*

Even the Psalmist declares the truth about the amazing power, (and protection) that the Fire of God brings and what it does to the Lord's enemies:

> *"**A fire goes before Him**, and burns up His enemies round about.*
> *His lightnings light the world; the earth sees and trembles.*
>
> *The mountains melt like wax at the Presence of the LORD, at*
> *the Presence of the Lord of the whole earth. The heavens declare*
> *His righteousness, and all the peoples see His glory!*
>
> *Let all be put to shame who serve carved images, who*
> *boast of idols. Worship Him, all you gods. (Psalm 97:3-7)*

King Nebuchadnezzar was astonished when he looked into the fiery furnace and saw not only the three servants of God; but now, he also saw a *fourth person!*

> *"…Did we not cast three men bound into the midst of the fire?"*
> *They answered and said to the king, "True, O king." "Look!"*
> *he answered, "I see four men loose, walking in the midst*
> *of the fire; and they are not hurt, and the form of the*
> *fourth is like **the Son of God.**" (Daniel 3:24, 25)*

King Nebuchadnezzar went near the mouth of the burning furnace and spoke:

> *"Shadrach, Meshach, and Abed-Nego, servants of the*
> *Most High God, come out, and come here." Then Shadrach,*
> *Meshach, and Abed-Nego came from the midst of the fire. And the*
> *satraps, administrators, governors, and the king's counselors*
> *gathered together, and they saw these men on whose bodies the fire*
> *had no power; the hair of their head was not singed nor were their*
> *garments affected, and the smell of fire was not on them.*

> *Nebuchadnezzar spoke, saying, "Blessed be the God of Shadrach,*
> *Meshach, and Abed-Nego, who sent **His Angel** and delivered*
> *His servants who trusted in Him, and they have frustrated the*
> *king's word, and yielded their bodies, that they should not serve*
> *nor worship any god except their own God! Therefore I make a*
> *decree that any people, nation, or language which speaks anything*
> *amiss against the God of Shadrach, Meshach, and Abed-Nego shall*
> *be cut in pieces, and their houses shall be made an ash heap; because*
> *there is no other God who can deliver like this." (Daniel 3:26-29)*

Then the King promoted Shadrach, Meshach, and Abednego in the province of Babylon.

The Fiery Presence of Christ came, in an amazing Christophony like fashion to protect Shadrach, Meshach, and Abednego in the midst of blazing furnace. It is quite possible that the same Holy Fire that protected Shadrach, Meshach, and Abednego also caused the ones who had thrown the servants of God into the furnace to perish instantly! We have already seen numerous occasions in the Bible where the Fire of God goes out before Him and burns up His enemies.

Shadrach, Meshach, and Abednego brought great honor and glory to God by trusting wholeheartedly in Him – even in the midst of intense testing. They kept the testimony of God even as they faced the fiery furnace!

It is fascinating to note that their original Hebrew names; Shadrach, Meshach, and Abednego had such relevant meaning to that which their lives would end up testifying:

    A. Hananiah: "God has favored."
    B. Mishael: "Who is that which God is."
    C. Azariah: "Jehovah has helped."

For God truly did show *favor* to these servants of His. God demonstrated His awesome power and Presence in the midst of a Holy Fire and declared to the people that day – *who He is*!

This was the same God who told Moses in a burning fire that His name was Jehovah (**the I AM**) who also came and delivered Shadrach, Meshach, and Abednego in their moment of trial.

He is God… The God of Holy Fire!

SHADRACH, MESHACH & ABEDNEGO IN THE FURNACE, WITH THE GOD OF HOLY FIRE

CHAPTER 10
A FIRE ON MT. ZION

Chapter 10
A Fire On Mt. Zion

The Lord has now appeared in Holy Fire on many mountains throughout the land of Israel. Just for review, we saw in Genesis the manifestation of God's Holy Presence come as a fiery torch or burning lamp - as His Holy Fire passed between the sacrifices that Abram laid before God on Mt. Hermon where the Lord sealed His Holy Covenant with Abram.

We read about the Holy Fire of God that was revealed to Moses at Mt. Sinai, which turned out to be the fiery Presence of the Eternal God who lives forever more, and that this God declared His name to be Jehovah (YHWH, I AM).

Then the Lord came in Holy Fire upon Mt. Carmel, as the prophet Elijah challenged the nation to witness who the true God in Israel was… Jehovah or Baal, as the Holy Fire of God's Presence, came and consumed Elijah's sacrifice – as the prophet declared that the Lord Jehovah – He is… "the God who *answers* by fire!"

The Holy Fire of God also fell upon Mt. Moriah, on the altar that King David had built, at the threshing floor of Ornan. Later at that same mountain location, David's son Solomon would build a Temple to bear the name of the Holy One of Israel, where once more the Holy Fire and Glory of God would come down at the Temple dedication and consume the sacrifices!

Mt. Zion is a portion of Mt. Moriah. Most people don't know that Mt. Moriah is actually several mountains clustered together including lower Mt. Moriah where Solomon's Temple was built, and upper Mt. Moriah which is the Mount of Olives!

"And he said, take now thy son, thine only son Isaac, whom thou lovest, and get thee into __the land of Moriah__; and offer him there for a burnt offering upon __one of the mountains__ which I will tell thee of." (Genesis 22:2)

God's eternal purposes concerning Mt. Zion did not begin with David! It began to unfold during the life of Abram some seven hundred years *before* King David was on Mt. Zion!

There was a Prophet–Priest–King called Melchizedek who reigned in Salem, which was ancient Jeru-**Salem**, (the same location (habitation) of Mt. Zion that David knew.

*"Then Melchizedek, **King of Salem**, brought out bread and wine; he was the priest of God Most High. And he blessed him and said: "Blessed be Abram of God Most High, **Possessor of Heaven and earth**; and blessed be God Most High, Who has delivered your enemies into your hand. "And he gave him a tithe of all."* (Genesis 14:18-20)

At this point in Abram's life, (Genesis chapter 14), Abram hadn't even received his covenant calling from God yet. The blessing, impartation, and prophecy from Melchizedek called Abram a *"Possessor of Heaven and Earth"* This prophecy was fulfilled in the next chapter (Genesis 15) when Abram encountered God, and received by a declaration from the Lord, his full destiny, and purpose!

God cut a covenant with Abram, telling him that his descendants would be as numerous as the stars and promised Abram an enormous amount of land for all of the families that would come forth as his offspring. God even changed Abram's name to Abraham that day! Abraham became the Father of the nation of Israel that day (spiritually), and through him, all families and nations of the earth would be greatly blessed! Melchizedek's prophecy came true… Abraham did become a Possessor of Heaven and Earth!

King Melchizedek had ministered that blessing to Abram from a *priestly stream*, with inspiration from God in a *prophetic stream*, under the declaration and authority of a *kingly stream*.

Melchizedek was a true Prophet-Priest-King, who reigned on Mt. Zion. He was the first priest ever mentioned in Scripture. There is no coincidence that his Throne was located upon Mt. Zion. There would come amazing parallels (and successions) between King Melchizedek, King David, and the coming King of Kings, Christ Jesus, who all would reign on Mt. Zion!

Now King David himself was also a Prophet-Priest-King, who like King Melchizedek, ruled and reigned on Mt. Zion! Looking at the life of David, the Bible confirms that David was:

A Prophet.

Both the Old and New Testament declares King David to be a prophet of God.

> *"Thus says David the son of Jesse; thus says the man raised up on high, the anointed of the God of Jacob, and the sweet*

psalmist of Israel: "The Spirit of the LORD spoke by me,
and His word was on my tongue." (2 Samuel 23:1, 2)

"Therefore, being a prophet, and knowing that God had sworn
with an oath to him that of the fruit of his body, according to the
flesh, He would raise up the Christ to sit on his Throne, he, foreseeing
this, spoke concerning the resurrection of the Christ, that His soul was
not left in Hades, nor did His flesh see corruption." (Acts 2:30, 31)

David recorded incredibly accurate and clear messianic prophecies about Christ nearly a thousand years beforehand!

A Priest.

It seems fairly clear from Scripture that David was a priest of God, but since he could not have been of the Aaronic Priesthood through the lineage of Aaron, how could this be? We know that David wore the linen ephod that *only* a high priest could wear…

"David was clothed with a robe of fine linen, as were all the
Levites who bore the ark, the singers, and Chenaniah the music
*master with the singers. **David also wore a linen ephod.**"*
(1 Chronicles 15:27)

There is perhaps a possible explanation that I submit to your consideration… Could David have been operating from the priestly, eternal order of Melchizedek? David prophesied profoundly to the Lord Jesus Christ Himself that He was also a part of the priestly order of Melchizedek. David obviously had some level of understanding concerning this priestly order. David received this revelation from Father God in Heaven and then prophesied it directly to Jesus. Here is what David said:

"The LORD (Father God) said to my Lord (Jesus),
"Sit at My right hand, till I make Your enemies Your
footstool. The LORD shall send the rod of Your strength
<u>out of Zion</u>. Rule in the midst of Your enemies!"

Your people shall be volunteers in the day of Your power;
In the beauties of holiness, from the womb of the morning,
You have the dew of Your youth. The LORD has sworn
And will not relent, <u>"You are a priest forever according</u>
<u>to the order of Melchizedek</u>." (Psalm 110)

If David were not a priest of the Most High God, how else could he have come into open view of the Holy Ark of God's Presence and not die as 70,000 others did, who just peered into the Ark?

How else could David sit before the Ark, and minister unto the Lord there, or as we said, wear the priestly linen ephod on several occasions, and even eat the priestly shewbread that were only for the priests of God?

A King.

David was anointed King of Israel when he was a young shepherd boy in Bethlehem by the prophet Samuel. It would take many years for that prophecy to come to pass, and even when it did, it took years from the beginning of its prophetic fulfillment to come to complete fruition.

As a Prophet-Priest-King, David loved Mt. Zion, for he knew by revelation, and the promise of God, that one day the Messiah would come and be enthroned on this very same mountain! Mt. Zion was the mountain of kings, but One was coming, who would reign there forever – the King of *all* Kings!

It was upon the Holy Hill of Mt. Zion that the Throne of David was established. It had great spiritual significance, and an unfolding prophetic destiny, because David's Throne there would become the very Throne that Jesus would eventually sit upon! A Throne without end! The Lord is coming back to Mt. Zion to rule the nations from there during His millennial reign!

"Yet I have set My King on My holy hill of Zion." (Psalm 2:6)

"See, I lay a stone in Zion, a chosen and precious cornerstone, and the one who trusts in Him will never be put to shame." (Isaiah 28:16)

"His foundation is in the holy mountains. the LORD loves the gates of Zion more than all the dwellings of Jacob. Glorious things are spoken of you,O city of God! Selah (Psalm 87:1-3)

The word "Zion" is mentioned over 150 times in the Bible. It means "sunny heights." Zion was first synonymous with "the city of David." It became the seat of power in Israel, and after Solomon's Temple was built there, its meaning grew to become understood as "the city of God."

In the Old Testament "Zion" referred figuratively to Israel, as the people of God, and the dwelling place of the Most High.

"…And they shall call you The City of the LORD, Zion of the Holy One of Israel." (Isaiah 60:14)

But in the New Testament, the meaning of "Zion" grew, even more, to refer to the *spiritual* Kingdom of God. It now includes all who have received Christ the King, and are a part of His Heavenly Kingdom (city).

"You have not come to a mountain that can be touched and that is burning with fire; to darkness, gloom and storm; to a

*trumpet blast or to such a voice speaking words that those who
heard it begged that no further word be spoken to them, because
they could not bear what was commanded: "If even an animal
touches the mountain, it must be stoned to death." The sight was
so terrifying that Moses said, "I am trembling with fear."*

___But you have come to Mount Zion, to the city of the living God,___
*the heavenly Jerusalem. You have come to thousands upon thousands
of angels in joyful assembly, to the church of the firstborn, whose
names are written in heaven. You have come to God, the Judge of all,
to the spirits of the righteous made perfect, to Jesus the mediator of
a new covenant, and to the sprinkled blood that speaks a better
word than the blood of Abel." (Hebrews 12:18-24)*

We can gain great understanding in the purposes of God
concerning Mt. Zion through the Book of Hebrews. That book
draws a significant contrast between Mt. Sinai and Mt. Zion.

The New Testament book of Hebrews is primarily a book about
two Covenants, the Old Covenant of God, represented by Mt.
Sinai, where the Law was given, and the New Covenant of
God, represented by Mt. Zion, which speaks of Grace. Hebrews
exhort the believer to leave Mt. Sinai behind, in favor of Mt.
Zion. At Mt. Zion, our hearts can know the Lord in a far deeper
way than anyone could at Mt. Sinai.

Under the old Law, relationship with God was based on a set
of laws and determined only by obedience. You received
blessings you obeyed (and curses if you did not!)

Israel proved how difficult it would be to try and live under
that type of restrictive lifestyle, for it was based on a rules
oriented relationship with God – but it did not transform the

human heart. But God had a better Covenant in mind to accomplish that very thing:

*"I will give you a new heart and put a new spirit
within you; I will take the heart of stone out of your flesh
and give you a heart of flesh."* (Ezekiel 36:26)

Under the New Covenant, the Holy Spirit came and made us *alive* unto God, flooding our hearts with His Spirit, and making us His dwelling place. We passed from death (dead works) unto life (eternal).

We were blessed with every manner of spiritual blessing in the heavenly places and seated with Christ (spiritually) in Heaven (Mt. Zion, the city of God,) or as Paul said in Galatians:

*"For it is written that Abraham had two sons: the one by
a bondwoman, the other by a freewoman. But he who was
of the bondwoman was born according to the flesh, and he
of the freewoman through promise, which things are symbolic.
For these are the two covenants: the one from Mount Sinai
which gives birth to bondage, which is Hagar — for this Hagar
is Mount Sinai in Arabia, and corresponds to Jerusalem which
now is, and is in bondage with her children — **but the Jerusalem
above** is free, which is the mother of us all."* (Galatians 4:22-26)

The New Covenant is therefore not based on our faithfulness to rules – but upon Christ faithfulness to us – to lead us away from Mt. Sinai, and up to Mt. Zion, as our citizenship is there!

*"For our citizenship is in Heaven, from which we also eagerly
wait for the Savior, the Lord Jesus Christ..."* (Philippians 3:20)

Does that mean we have no responsibilities in God to attend to Godly behavior? Of course, not! Take the Book of Ephesians for example. The first three chapters of Ephesians speak of what the faithfulness of Christ has procured for us, but in the last three chapters, Paul gives clears commands for Godly behavior. Take for instance how wives are to submit to their husbands, children need to obey their parents, and we *all* must submit to the authorities we are under, etc.

The New Covenant does not begin with commands; it begins with Christ! Obedience for us is trusting in the faithfulness of Christ to help us do what we could never accomplish on our own. Living a Godly life, that is covered in His Righteous, and not our own!

Therefore, coming to maturity in our Christian walk and our relationship with Christ is akin to *coming up* to Mt. Zion. The more we grow – the higher we go!

The Prophet Isaiah prophesied in Isaiah 4 with linear fashion, concerning Mt. Zion, and the coming Branch (Government) of the Lord Jesus Christ – almost 700 years beforehand! His prophecy spoke directly into the birth and Kingdom ministry of our Lord!

"In that day, the Branch of the LORD shall be beautiful and glorious; and the fruit of the earth shall be excellent and appealing for those of Israel who have escaped.

*And it shall come to pass that he who is left in Zion and remains in Jerusalem will be called holy—everyone who is **recorded** among the living in Jerusalem. When the Lord has washed away the filth of the daughters of Zion, and purged the blood of Jerusalem from her midst, by the spirit of judgment and by the spirit of burning, then the LORD will create above*

139

every dwelling place of Mount Zion, and above her assemblies, a
cloud and smoke by day and the shining of a flaming fire by night.
For over all the glory there will be a covering. And there will be
a tabernacle for shade in the daytime from the heat, for a place of
refuge, and for a shelter from storm and rain." (Isaiah 4:2-6)

Isaiah prophesied that the powerful role of the Holy Spirit would come in the *spirit of judgment* and the *spirit of burning* – in both instances the Hebrew word Isaiah used for *spirit* there was the word *ruwach*, referring the Spirit of God!

The prophet Isaiah was declaring that the filth of Israel's sin needed to be purged before the Shekinah Glory would come and fill their tabernacles and assemblies.

A Holy Fire was beginning to burn upon Mt. Zion. To come up to Mt. Zion meant preparing to embrace the process of purification. The cleansing fire of God was to come upon the sons and daughters of God!

The Lord came and washed away the filth of daughters of Zion, to all who received Him!

Eventually, through the atoning work of the cross, and His substitutionary death, the Lord, even purged the blood curse of Jerusalem, the city who killed so many Holy Prophets of God (including Jesus).

"Jerusalem, Jerusalem, you who kill the prophets and
stone those sent to you, how often I have longed to
gather your children together, as a hen gathers her chicks
under her wings, and you were not willing." (Matthew 23:37)

We know the Lord purged the blood of Jerusalem because at the cross He asked the Father to forgive them Shall the Father not honor the intercession of His Son?

The Lord also understood that He must go away, in order to send His Holy Spirit back to empower His people and birth the New Testament Church! Jesus built a bridge between natural Mt. Zion up to the Heavenly Mt. Zion!

Yet there is still significant prophetic purpose and destiny that will be fulfilled on natural Mt. Zion concerning end–time purposes according to Scripture. Our King Jesus is going to come back and rule and reign in the nations for a thousand years on that Holy Mountain!

> *"Then the moon will be disgraced, and the sun ashamed;*
> *For the LORD of hosts **will reign on Mount Zion** and in*
> *Jerusalem, before His elders, gloriously."* (Isaiah 24:23)

> *"I will make the lame a remnant, and the outcast a strong*
> *nation; so the LORD **will reign over them in Mount Zion***
> *From now on, even forever."* (Micah 4:7)

To as many as received the Gospel message of Jesus Christ, they were washed by His Word, cleansed by His blood, and sanctified by the Holy Spirit!

And when the Holy Spirit was finally poured out upon the 120 in the upper room, which was called The Cenacle – where do you think that happened? It happened (of course) on Mt. Zion!

FOLLOW THE LION
UP TO MT. ZION !!!

CHAPTER ELEVEN
COMETH THE
BAPTIZER OF FIRE

Chapter Eleven
Cometh The Baptizer of Fire

Four hundred years came and went since the last recorded words of the Holy Prophets of God. The Old Testament concluded with the words of Malachi, whose name means "Messenger of God." Malachi was the last of the 12 minor prophets. In the closing words of the Old Testament, Malachi prophesied that God was about to send forth a messenger (John the Baptist), who would prepare the way for the Lord to come suddenly to His Temple, in order to establish a New Covenant!

> "Behold, I send My messenger, and he will prepare
> the way before Me. And the Lord, whom you seek,
> will suddenly come to His Temple, even **the Messenger
> of the Covenant**, in whom you delight. Behold, He is
> coming, says the LORD of Hosts." (Malachi 3:1)

Malachi makes very clear, the *purpose* of the coming Messiah, was not only to bring us a New Covenant but also to purify His sons and daughters, through the Holy Fire of God! He refers to Jesus as *"The Messenger(Angel) of the Covenant."*

> "But who can endure the day of His coming? And who
> can stand when He appears? **For He is like a refiner's fire**
> And like launderers' soap. He will sit as a refiner and a
> purifier of silver; He will purify the sons of Levi, and purge
> them as gold and silver, that they may offer to the LORD
> an offering in righteousness." (Malachi 3:2, 3)

The prophetic ministry of John the Baptist was foretold not only by the prophet Malachi but by the prophet Isaiah as well:

> *"The voice of one crying in the wilderness: "Prepare the way of the LORD; make straight in the desert, a highway for our God. Every valley shall be exalted, and every mountain and hill brought low; the crooked places shall be made straight, and the rough places smooth; the Glory of the LORD shall be revealed, and all flesh shall see it together; for the mouth of the LORD has spoken." (Isaiah 40:3-5)*

John the Baptist was born a Nazarite, from the priestly lineage of his father Zacharias, down through the priestly course of Abia. He preached in the wilderness of Judea, a message of repentance from sin through baptism (immersion).

He also continually declared that One (Messiah) far greater than himself was coming and that He would bring a much more powerful baptism. John prophesied that when Jesus came, He would baptize them in the Holy Spirit – and Fire!

> *"I indeed baptize you with water unto repentance, but He who is coming after me is mightier than I, whose sandals I am not worthy to carry. **He will baptize you with the Holy Spirit and fire**. His winnowing fan is in His hand, and He will thoroughly clean out His threshing floor, and gather His wheat into the barn; but He will burn up the chaff with unquenchable fire." (Matthew 3:11, 12)*

John the Baptist was used mightily of God in preparing the way for the King of Holy Fire. We have seen throughout the Old Testament Jesus coming many times in manifestation of Holy Fire, now Jesus is about to fulfill His mission of fire on earth!

The prophetic message of John, the Baptist concerning Jesus, was so important that Jesus declared that there was no greater

Old Testament prophet born of women – than John the Baptist!

At the perfect moment, Jesus appeared to John the Baptist at the river Jordan and requested John to baptize Him. John was astonished, knowing that Jesus was bringing a baptism far greater than anything he was ministering. So John was transparent with Jesus, exclaiming:

*"**I need to be baptized by You**, and are You coming to me?" But Jesus answered and said to him, "Permit it to be so now, for thus it is fitting for us to fulfill all righteousness." Then he allowed Him. When He had been baptized, Jesus came up immediately from the water; and behold, the heavens were opened to Him, and He saw the Spirit of God descending like a dove and alighting upon Him. And suddenly a voice came from Heaven, saying, "This is My Beloved Son, in whom I am well pleased." (Matthew 3:13-17)*

The Book of Luke says that immediately after this, the Spirit drove Jesus into the Judean wilderness, where He fasted for forty days and forty nights. Near the end of that fast, Jesus endured severe testing from the Satan but overcame him. The Bible says that after that deep testing, this was the result:

*"Then Jesus returned **in the power of the Spirit** to Galilee, and news of Him went out through all the surrounding region. And He taught in their synagogues, being glorified by all." (Luke 4:14, 15)*

Thus, the power ministry of Jesus began. It all started with the impartation of the Holy Spirit upon Jesus at the Jordan River with John the Baptist. That empowerment from the Holy Ghost enabled Jesus to endure the severe testing in the desert, and then launched Him into a power signs and wonders ministry!

*"...God anointed Jesus of Nazareth **with the Holy Spirit and with power**, who went about doing good and healing all who were oppressed by the devil, for God was with Him."* (Acts 10:38)

Jesus came preaching that the Kingdom of God was near, even at hand (within reach). He challenged the people to repent and believe in the Gospel! He didn't mince words, He confronted people with Love, but also with deliberate, and truthful piercing, and yet with compassion!

The people were astonished because He spoke with such *authority*. He exposed the deceit, arrogance, and religiosity of the Pharisees and Sadducees. Matthew 23 is a blistering indictment against those religious leaders. Here are just a few verses! Remember this is Jesus talking, our *Gentle Shepherd*!

"But woe to you, scribes and Pharisees, hypocrites! For you shut up the kingdom of Heaven against men; for you neither go in yourselves, nor do you allow those who are entering to go in." (Matthew 23:13)

"Woe to you, scribes and Pharisees, hypocrites! For you devour widows' houses, and for a pretense make long prayers. Therefore, you will receive greater condemnation." (Matthew 23:14)

"Woe to you, scribes and Pharisees, hypocrites! For you travel land and sea to win one proselyte, and when he is won, you make him twice as much a son of hell as yourselves." (Matthew 23:15)

"Woe to you, scribes and Pharisees, hypocrites! For you are like whitewashed tombs which indeed appear beautiful outwardly, but inside are full of dead men's bones and all uncleanness. Even so you also outwardly appear righteous to men, but inside you are full of hypocrisy and lawlessness." (Matthew 23:27)

"Woe to you, scribes and Pharisees, hypocrites! For you cleanse the outside of the cup and dish, but inside you are full of extortion and self-indulgence. Blind Pharisee, first cleanse the inside of the cup and dish, that the outside of them may be clean also." (Matthew 23:25, 26)

Jesus spoke very clearly, and often about hell. It is a message we don't hear a lot about today. The Lord brought such clear preaching on the matter; He emphatically declared to the people the criticality of receiving the Gospel of the Kingdom. He illustrated it be saying:

*"If your hand causes you to sin, cut it off. It is better for you to enter into life maimed, rather than having two hands, to go to hell, **into the fire that shall never be quenched." (Mark 9:43)***

*"And if your foot causes you to sin, cut it off. It is better for you to enter life lame, rather than having two feet, to be cast into hell, **into the fire that shall never be quenched." (Mark 9:45)***

*"And if your eye causes you to sin, pluck it out. It is better for you to enter the kingdom of God with one eye, rather than having two eyes, **and be cast into hell fire." (Mark 9:47)***

As Jesus was teaching from the 9th Chapter of Mark, He closed with this important truth:

*"**<u>For everyone will be seasoned with fire</u>** and every sacrifice will be seasoned with salt. Salt is good, but if the salt loses its flavor, how will you season it?" (Mark 9:49, 50)*

The Lord was bringing forth an imperative illustration here concerning the importance of the Holy Fire of God. He says that everyone will be *"salted (seasoned) with fire."* Salt is a preservative from corruption and decay. Fire purifies. We must be salted with Holy Fire!

The Lord is revealing here the importance of allowing His Holy Fire to come and purify His people from corrupt, carnal living in this life, and preserve them, rather than eventually perishing in the eternal fire of God, reserved of those who reject Him.

*"For God so loved the world that He gave His only begotten Son, that whoever believes in Him **should not perish** but have everlasting life. For God did not send His Son into the world to condemn the world, but that the world through Him might be saved." (John 3:16, 17)*

Jesus made it very clear, why He came! The Lord Jesus came with a mission of Holy Fire!

*"**I came to bring fire on the earth**, and how I wish it were already kindled!" (Luke 12:49)*

The Fire of God comes in blessing or judgment. It can come and cleanse, purify and preserve us now, in this life, or it can become the substance of eternal judgment in the hereafter.

"The ax is already at the root of the trees, and every tree that does not produce good fruit will be cut down and thrown into the fire." (Matthew 3:10)

"His winnowing fork is in his hand, and he will clear his threshing floor, gathering his wheat into the barn and burning up the chaff with unquenchable fire." (Matthew 3:12)

In the New Testament, water baptism was practiced by John the Baptist, the disciples of Jesus, and by Jesus Himself. It was not just a symbolic act of making an outward sign of an inward work through public confession, but rather a substantial doctrine in the faith of the believer, commanded by Jesus:

*"Go therefore and make disciples of all nations, **baptizing** them in the name of the Father and of the Son and of the Holy Spirit, and teaching them to obey everything that I have commanded you. And remember, I am with you always, to the end of the age."* (Matthew 28:19, 20)

Water baptism was the first stage of cleansing a new believer, with powerful spiritual dynamics at work, whereupon the person is identifying with and plunging into the very death, burial and resurrection of Jesus Christ!

The old, carnal nature (self-life) of the believer is plunged into the waters of baptism and buried there. When they arise out of the waters, they come up with their new nature, that is the life of Christ living in them. The outer man is shed like a snakeskin.

"Or do you not know that as many of us as were baptized into Christ Jesus were baptized into His death? Therefore we were buried with Him through baptism into death, that just as Christ was raised from the dead by the glory of the Father, even so we also should walk in newness of life. For if we have been united together in the likeness of His death, certainly we also shall be in the likeness of His resurrection, knowing this, that our old man was crucified with Him, that the body of sin might be done away with, that we should no longer be slaves of sin." (Romans 6: 3-6)

We will discuss in much greater detail the workings of the Baptism of the Holy Spirit in the next chapter. Suffice to say that Baptism is the next stage of cleansing and renewing our lives, by the indwelling life of the Holy Spirit.

The Holy Spirit is the Spirit of Truth and leads us into partaking of the Divine nature of God in our behavior, lifestyle, and brings us the mind of Christ, cleansing our hearts and minds, as well as our thoughts and beliefs...

We are now continually being led into Truth, delivered from falsehood and have become the dwelling (habitation) place of God. We are being brought to maturity through the Living Word of God and the dynamic power of the Holy Spirit's developmental work in our lives.

But John the Baptist prophesied that Jesus would baptize us, not only in the Holy Spirit but also with fire! What is the Baptism of Fire —and how do we get it?

The Baptism of the Holy Spirit is a baptism of Truth, that is, the indwelling life of the Holy Spirit and Truth coming to live inside us. **The Baptism of Fire is a baptism of Love!**

> *"Set me as a seal upon Your heart, as a seal upon Your arm;*
> *For Love is as strong as death, jealousy as cruel as the grave,*
> ***Its flames are flames of fire, a most vehement flame!***
> *Many waters cannot quench love, nor can the floods drown it.*
> *If a man would give for love all the wealth of his house,*
> *It would be utterly despised." (Songs of Solomon 8:6, 7)*

It seems unusual that the Word of God would use the word *"vehement flame"* to describe such passionate love. The Hebrew word used here there is *shalhebeth* and it literally means the fiery flame of Jehovah (YHWH, I AM) Himself!

It is the pure and Holy Fire of God's Love! Far beyond the essence of *phileo* love, and far more passionate than *eros* love, this vehement fire is the jealous Fire of God! *Agape' Love!*

A jealous God? It is important to understand the Hebrew word for jealous which is *quanna'*. It is used of God to mean *"not bearing any rival."*

"...for you shall worship no other god, for the LORD, whose name is Jealous, is a jealous God." (Exodus 34:14)

"For the LORD your God is a consuming fire, a jealous God." (Deuteronomy 4:24)

The Fire of God's Love is a vehement flame! He wants to seal His Love in our hearts and cleanse and purify us from all other lovers (idols). It is a difficult process that often takes many, many years of burning in the Holy Fire of God to consume all of those other *"rivals'* that compete with God for our affection.

As humans, we are a mixture of good and evil loves and motives. Self-interests, worldly passions, and carnal desires hold us at bay from the all–consuming fire of God that He wants to burn in us. God will burn anything we give Him!

Whereas Water Baptism begins to address *our fallen nature*, making us alive unto God from dead works; and the Baptism of the Holy Spirit begins to cleanse and purify *our minds* with Truth, the Baptism of Fire cleanses <u>*our hearts*</u> that is… our loves, desires, and motives so that we come to the place where we no longer *want* those evil things. We only want the Lord's abiding Presence! We become laid–down lovers of Jesus Christ alone!

This precious *Baptism of Divine Love* burns away all those selfish, evil and greedy desires, enabling us to more fully give our hearts over to the Bridegroom King. As the Fire of God intensifies in our lives, all the earthly pleasures we used to derive from evil deeds began to burn away — and the Lord increasingly becomes our *only* desire.

This process of purification by Holy Fire is not easy… It is often accompanied by repeated times of testing, trials, and suffering.

The painful process comes with much burning. Burning away the chaff from our lives, trials by fire, and learning to live life in a crucible of intense heat that has its purpose... to draw forth all the dross from our lives to the top, as in purifying gold.

The cleansing of our heart in the fire of Divine Love purges our selfish desires and motives, making us more bondable to Jesus!

Jesus Himself went through a very difficult "Baptism of Fire" process, intentionally directed by Father God, to fully prepare Him for some of the ultimate showdowns in His life.

> "...Who, in the days of His flesh, when He had offered up prayers and supplications, **with vehement cries and tears** to Him who was able to save Him from death, and was heard because of His godly fear, though He was a Son, yet **He learned obedience by the things which He suffered.**" (Hebrews 5:7, 8)

The forty days in the wilderness, the temptations of Satan, rejection, accusations, the Garden of Gethsemane, whippings, scourging's, beatings — and above all, the agony of the cross.

The *Baptism of Fire* in own His life helped fully prepare Jesus to override His own will and painstakingly embrace the will of His Father in obedience. Jesus said that this was a *"baptism."*

> "But I have a **Baptism to be baptized with**, and how distressed I am till it is accomplished!" (Luke 12:50)

This process, although very costly in our lives, yields the highest-level rewards, benefits, and even Glory, both now and in the life to come! It produces true faith, breaking our trust and dependence on everything other than Christ, and our faith is then more precious than gold!

"In this you greatly rejoice, though now for a little while, if need be, you have been grieved by various trials, that the genuineness of your faith, being much more precious than gold that perishes, though it is tested by fire, may be found to praise, honor, and glory at the revelation of Jesus Christ, whom having not seen you love." (1 Peter 1:6, 7)

"For our light affliction, which is but for a moment, is working for us a far more exceeding and eternal weight of glory." (2 Corinthians 4:17)

"For you, O God, tested us: you refined us like silver.
You brought us into prison and laid burdens on our backs.
You let men ride over or heads; we went through fire and water,
but you brought us to a place of abundance." (Psalms 66:10-12)

A Baptism of Fire can be quite discouraging if you are looking at it from a *short-ranged* lens. But if you can view each trial, temptation and situation (hardship) the Lord either produces (or allows) to come into your life —with an eternal (Heavenly perspective) it can make all the difference in the world!

Paul got the revelation of this and came to the realization that this was the secret path to the deepest intimacy into Divine Love with the Lord. Once he understood this — he pressed into Christ all the more! Paul came to the point — where he would not be denied!

"That I might know him, and the power of his resurrection, and the **fellowship of his sufferings**; *being made conformable to his death"*
(Philippians 3:10)

Paul would end up suffering tremendous adverse situations through shipwrecks, stoning's, beatings, and afflictions of body and soul. But in all this, Paul declared that he would joyfully suffer the loss of all things. In triumph over all these personal sufferings, Paul proclaimed:

"I reckon that the sufferings of this present time are not worthy to be compared with the glory which shall be revealed in us." (Romans 8:18)."

We must pursue the Baptizer of Fire! Jesus Christ!

What a precious process! We are first Baptized in water, dealing with the outer man and the beginning of the process of *regeneration,* so we began a whole new life in Christ — as we become a whole new creature — like the transformation of a caterpillar to a butterfly! *Metamorphosis!*

Then we receive the precious Baptism of the Holy Spirit that empowers us by transforming our mind, will and emotions, and leads us in newness of life, intercession, and service to God through the impartation of gifts and graces that He gives to us to help edify the Church.

Then comes the Baptism of Fire to those who lay everything on the altar of God! They come to that deep place of surrender and abandonment to God. Their lives become truly filled with the life of Christ — so that it's no longer they who live, but Christ who lives in them, and the life they now live, they live, *by faith,* in the Son of God! The Holy Fire of God burns in them day and night! The fiery flame of Jehovah (YHWH, I AM) inside them!

Their lives of obedience, submission, intimacy, and faith will reward them to experience and possess the very Glory of God, and they will reign with Him forever!

*"…We are heirs—heirs of God and co-heirs with Christ, if indeed we share in his sufferings, we shall also **share in His Glory**." (Romans 8:17)*

*"If we suffer with Him, we shall also **reign** with Him."*
(2 Timothy 2:12)

CHAPTER TWELVE
THE FIRE OF
PENTECOST

Chapter Twelve
The Fire of Pentecost

Jesus had accomplished the complete and perfect will of His Father during His earthly life, having lived a sin-free, righteous life, and then choosing to sacrifice that pure and precious life at Golgotha through an agonizing death on the cross — in our place, while the Father turned away His eyes from His Son because:

> *"You are of purer eyes than to behold evil,*
> *And cannot look upon wickedness." (Habakkuk 1:13)*

The Bible says that He who knew no sin, *became* sin, having taken all our sins upon Himself.

> *"For our sake, He made Him **to be sin** who knew no sin, so that in Him*
> *we might become the righteousness of God." (2 Corinthians 5:21)*

It was necessary for Jesus to die such a horrible death so that the curse of sin and death could be broken once and for all, and Jesus could become the Mediator of a New Covenant and a much better Covenant for us.

We can now enter into the Holy of Holies in a new and living way, by the blood of Jesus. Through repentance and faith towards Christ, we have been exonerated from the wrath of God and the penalty of death (for the wages of sin —is death). We have passed from death — unto life!

Jesus explained why His death, and leaving this earth was so important. Jesus purchased the Church with His own Blood. Now the plan of God was to empower the Church and create a glorious dwelling place for His Presence to come and abide. Man was to become the Temple of God through the Holy Spirit!

> *Nevertheless, I tell you the truth. It is to your advantage*
> *that I go away; for if I do not go away, the Helper will not*
> *come to you; but if I depart, I will send Him to you. And when*
> *He has come, He will convict the world of sin, and of righteousness,*
> *and of judgment: of sin, because they do not believe in Me; of*
> *righteousness, because I go to My Father and you see Me no*
> *more; of judgment, because the ruler of this world is judged.*

> *"I still have many things to say to you, but you cannot bear them*
> *now. However, when He, the Spirit of Truth, has come, He will*
> *guide you into all truth; for He will not speak on His own authority,*
> *but whatever He hears He will speak; and He will tell you things to*
> *come. He will glorify Me, for He will take of what is Mine and declare*
> *it to you. All things that the Father has are Mine. Therefore, I said*
> *that He will take of Mine and declare it to you." (John16:7-15)*

Let's follow this storyline in the Word of God concerning the events leading up to the outpouring of the Holy Spirit at Pentecost, — starting from the time of the death of Jesus.

We know the moment that Jesus died, that He descended into Hell. But Why? First of all, to fulfill <u>all</u> of righteousness, for He had to receive the same just punishment as a mortal man. Remember that Jesus was 100% God, but He was *also* 100% man, and He had taken upon Himself the sins of the world.

Jesus fulfilled the righteous requirement of the Word of God and all spiritual legalities by dying with the sin of the world upon Him (*for the soul that sinneth shall die*) and carrying the curse of sin – that 100% man portion (the sin portion) to Hades.

Both the Old and New Testaments declared Jesus would go Hades... but, (most importantly) He would not be *left* there!

*"...he, foreseeing this, spoke concerning the resurrection of the Christ, that His soul was not **left** in Hades, nor did His flesh see corruption."*
(Acts 2:31)

*"For You will not **leave** My soul in Sheol, nor will You allow Your Holy One to see corruption." (Psalm 16:10*

Second, having concluded that final portion of conquering sin once and for all by taking it to hell, the Scriptures tells us Jesus then proclaimed His great victory to the spirits (fallen angels) in prison there in Hades.

*"For Christ also suffered once for sins, the righteous for the unrighteous, that He might bring us to God, being put to death in the flesh but made alive in the spirit, in which He went and proclaimed to **the spirits in prison**, because they formerly did not obey..." (1 Peter 3:18-20)*

Third, He was there as 100% God who had just conquered sin, and the curse of Hell and Death and took those very keys back from Satan in great victory!

*"I am He who lives, and **was dead**, and behold, I am alive forevermore. Amen. **And I have the keys of Hades and of Death.**" (Revelation 1:18)*

Hell, or Hades in the New Testament was also called Sheol in the Old Testament, the valley of the dead. It is a gruesome place. We need to be reminded what the Bible says about Sheol:

It is a prison of souls with gates and bars.

*"I said, in the middle of my days, I must depart; I am consigned to the **gates** of Sheol for the rest of my years." (Isaiah 38:10)*

161

> *"Will it go down to the **bars** of Sheol? Shall we
> descend together into the dust?"* *(Job 17:16)*

It is a place of darkness.

> *"Sheol beneath is stirred up to meet you when you come; it rouses
> the **shades** to greet you, all who were leaders of the earth; it raises
> from their thrones all who were kings of the nations."* *(Isaiah 14:9)*

It is a place where no work is done – and no wisdom exists.

> *"for there is no work or thought or knowledge or wisdom
> in Sheol, to which you are going."* *(Ecclesiastes 9:10)*

Most frightening of all... It is a place where no one praises God!

> *"For in death there is no remembrance of you;
> in Sheol who will give you **praise**?"* *(Psalm 6:5)*

> *"The dead do not **praise** the LORD, nor any who
> go down into silence."* *(Psalm 115:17)*

> *"For Sheol does not thank you; death does not
> **praise** you; those who go down to the pit do not
> hope for your faithfulness."* *(Isaiah 38:18)*

Fourth, Jesus then crossed over the great divide (chasm), to *Paradise*, the Eden of God, which was also called *Abraham's bosom*. It was the place where He promised one of the thieves dying on a cross next to Him, that they *both* would be in *Paradise* later that very day. It was a place where the righteous in God were awaiting their triumphal ascent into Heaven, led by Jesus! I can only imagine their rejoicing to see King Jesus triumphant!

It is amazing that though Jesus was 100% God, He chose to empty Himself of Deity (Divine privilege) while on the earth.

> *"Who, being in very nature God, did not consider*
> *equality with God something to be used to His own advantage;*
> *rather He made Himself nothing by taking the very nature of a*
> *servant being made in human likeness. And being found in*
> *appearance as a man, He humbled Himself by becoming obedient*
> *to death— even death on a cross!" (Philippians 2:6-8)*

Everything Jesus did upon the earth, He did *as* 100% man, who *was* 100% yielded to the Holy Spirit. Because He was 100% man, He followed every step of righteousness that a man would need to follow. That's why John the Baptist was so surprised when Jesus, the sinless Son of God asked him to baptize Him — but Jesus said it was necessary to fulfill *all* of righteousness, the man portion of Jesus.

That is why it was necessary for Jesus, who died as a propitiation for our sins, had to carry out the full sentence (penalty) for sin; had to experience death and carry the sin of the world to Hades. The Bible says that later, when Jesus re-entered Heaven, that He even *passed* through His own Blood!

> *"Not with the blood of goats and calves, **but with***
> ***His own blood** He entered the Most Holy Place once for all,*
> *having obtained eternal redemption." (Hebrews 9:12)*

When Jesus arose from the grave on the third day, He still had important, unfinished business upon the earth to accomplish before His Glorious Ascension!

He established proof of His resurrection, appearing to Mary Magdalene first, then to His disciples, and eventually to some 400 people! But He wanted to prove to them that it was truly Him — back from the dead, and *still* 100% man and 100% God!

To prove that He was the same man in flesh and blood, Christ Jesus encouraged them to examine His nail-pierced hands and His body. To further prove His restored flesh — He asked them for food, and He ate with them!

> *"Now as they said these things, Jesus Himself stood in the midst of them, and said to them, "Peace to you." But they were terrified and frightened, and supposed they had seen a spirit. And He said to them, "Why are you troubled? And why do doubts arise in your hearts? Behold My hands and My feet, that it is I Myself. Handle Me and see, for a spirit does not have flesh and bones as you see I have."*
>
> *When He had said this, He showed them His hands and His feet. But while they still did not believe for joy, and marveled, He said to them, "Have you any food here?" So they gave Him a piece of a broiled fish and some honeycomb. And He took it and ate in their presence."*
> *(Luke 24:36-43)*

Jesus spent about 40 days upon the earth after His resurrection, but the time came for His Glorious Ascension into Heaven, for Jesus did it, He paid it all! He knew He was about to return to His Father. He wanted the disciples to know something very important was about to happen. Jesus *last words* on earth were:

> *"And being assembled together with them, He commanded them not to depart from Jerusalem, but to wait for the Promise of the Father, "which," He said, "you have heard from Me; for*

*John truly baptized with water, but **you shall be baptized
with the Holy Spirit** not many days from now."* (Acts 1:6)

*"But **you shall receive power when the Holy Spirit has come
upon you**; and you shall be witnesses to Me in Jerusalem, and
in all Judea and Samaria, and to the end of the earth."* (Acts 1:8)

After saying those very words, Jesus was taken up in a cloud,
and disappeared from their site! The disciples had no clue as
to what was about to be released from Heaven a few days later!

Again, everything Jesus did in His earthly ministry was done
directly through the revelation, power, and reliance on the
Holy Spirit, for Jesus said:

*"Then Jesus answered and said to them, "Most assuredly, I say to you,
the Son can **do nothing of Himself**, but what He sees the Father do;
for whatever He does, the Son also does in like manner."* (John 5:19)

Jesus went on to demonstrate to us that everything He did was
done as a natural man (because Jesus had emptied Himself of
the right to use His Deity to perform miracles). His ministry
was as a person like you or me, fully yielded to God in the Holy
Spirit and that it was the power of the Holy Spirit working
through Jesus who performed all the miracles:

*"But if I cast out demons **by the Spirit of God**, surely the
kingdom of God has come upon you."* (Matthew 12:28)

Jesus was the perfect role model of how to walk in a powerful
ministry upon the earth as a natural human being, through the
power of the Holy Spirit. In every way, He set a precedent!

Now, that precious Holy Spirit was about to be given to the Church. What an incredible moment in the history of mankind!

The word Pentecost means the "fiftieth day." It originated in the Old Testament as a Jewish Holiday to commemorate one of the feasts or High Holidays — seven weeks after Passover.

This Holiday was known as the "Festival of Weeks" or *Shavuot*. It was originally a harvest festival (Exodus 23:16), but in time turned to commemorate the giving of the law on Mt. Sinai.

There is a very important distinction here, or correlation — the Law was given on Mt. Sinai *at* Pentecost, while the Holy Spirit was poured out in the upper room on Mt. Zion *at* Pentecost.

Two mountains of Holy Fire — one the mountain of laws (Sinai), and the other, the mountain of Grace (Zion). Heaven came down on both with Fire — on the same day of Pentecost!

Jesus death was the fulfillment of the Feast of Passover, the day He died. He spent three days in the bowels of the earth, then 40 days on earth before His ascension. So around the 43rd day, at the ascension of Jesus, He told His disciples to wait in Jerusalem for the Promise of the Holy Spirit — that would come… not many days from then. It happened, just as Jesus said, about one week later — on the 50th day after Passover!

About 120 people were gathered in an upper room, all in one accord. Suddenly there was the sound of a mighty rushing wind! It filled the whole house where they were assembled.

Then the most amazing thing happened! Cloven tongues of **Holy Fire** set down upon each person there! They were suddenly filled with the Holy Spirit — and began to speak in other tongues (languages) as the Holy Spirit gave utterance!

There were men dwelling there from many different nations of the earth, and they all marveled because they were hearing those who had been filled with the Holy Spirit — speaking in their native tongues from that nation they came from!

They were astonished because they knew these people were local natives and could not have known the very languages they were speaking! Even more amazing than that was *what* they were saying, under the influence of the Holy Spirit:

> *"...Look, are not all these who speak Galileans? And how is it that we hear, each in our own language in which we were born? Parthians and Medes and Elamites, those dwelling in Mesopotamia, Judea and Cappadocia, Pontus and Asia, Phrygia and Pamphylia, Egypt and the parts of Libya adjoining Cyrene, visitors from Rome, both Jews and proselytes, Cretans and Arabs—we **hear them speaking in our own** tongues **the wonderful works of God**." So they were all amazed and perplexed, saying to one another, "Whatever could this mean?"*
> *(Acts 2:7-12)*

At that moment, the New Testament Church was birthed for all nations! Peter delivered an incredible message of how death could not hold Christ Jesus in Hades, and how God raised Him up to sit upon the Throne — at the right hand of God!

Peter also confirmed that this outpouring was the prophetic fulfillment of the Book of Joel where the prophet had said:

> *"And it shall come to pass in the last days, says God, that I will pour out of My Spirit on all flesh; your sons and*

your daughters shall prophesy, your young men shall see
visions, your old men shall dream dreams. And on My
menservants and on My maidservants I will pour out My
Spirit in those days; and they shall prophesy." (Acts 2:17, 18)

Peter's message cut to the heart of the people and that day some three thousand souls got saved! The Church began to grow, as the people continued steadfastly in the apostle's doctrine and fellowship, breaking bread — and prayers!

Fear came upon every soul, and many signs and wonders were performed through the apostles. There was a strong sense of community, as the people held all things in common, selling their possessions and goods and dividing them among all the people — as anyone had a need.

The Holy Fire of God that was once dwelled on Mt. Sinai, lead the children of Israel through the wilderness, and then fell upon the House of God at the dedication of Solomon's Temple — had now come to *live* inside of the hearts of men!

THE HOLY FIRE OF PENTECOST!

CHAPTER THIRTEEN
THE REFINER'S FIRE

Chapter Thirteen
The Refiner's Fire

Living a victorious Christian life is no easy matter. There are constant struggles and battles from numerous outer forces that constantly assail us on every side, and then there is the war within us...

First, we are born with a sin nature, then as we grow from toddler to teen, it grows with us. We develop a self–life that wants to be recognized, appreciated, and a pleasure center (sin life) inside us that takes on a whole life of its own. The Bible says we become enslaved to sin and it has mastery over us.

Left unchecked, we enter our adult lives, bound by sin and selfishness. We grow up into an unrighteous lifestyle while living in a sensuous and pornographic society, with sexual images and innuendos — that bombard us everywhere we turn. Our minds and hearts are intentionally saturated in unholy, and unrighteous values trying to permeate our senses (eye–gates, and ear–gates) daily.

It is not by accident. There are two forces that are vying for your affection(s). There are two Fathers. One is Father God, the Father of Truth, and the other is Satan, the Father of Lies. Both Fathers want *you* to do their will. Both are constantly at work in your life —whether you know it or not!

Father God, who the Bible refers to as Abba Father (Daddy), is seeking your adoption (return) back to His family for eternity, from Whom we were separated because of the fall of man (Adam).

Father God did this through the atoning, and redemptive work of His Son Jesus through the cross! Our God is intent on raising up sons like unto His own, and bringing *"many sons (and daughters) into Glory!"* (Hebrews 2:10).

> *"But when the set time had fully come, God sent his Son, born of a woman, born under the law, to redeem those under the law, that we might receive adoption to sonship, because you are his sons, God sent the Spirit of His Son into our hearts, the Spirit who calls out, "Abba Father." So you are* **no longer a slave**, *but God's child; and since you are his child, God has made you also an heir."* (Galatians 4:4-7)

The Father of Lies is an opportunist who tries to leverage every advantage in the world to keep you living in your fallen nature (sin–life), through selfishness and pleasure–seeking. His ultimate goal is to claim you at the end of your life — to spend eternity with him where there is weeping and gnashing of teeth, that is in Hell, the eternal place God prepared for the Devil and his Angels.

These two Fathers are complete opposites. One is pure and Holy – the other is evil and wicked. They both are trying to birth their will in your life. They both want you to fulfill their *desires*. The meaning of the word "desire" is quite amazing:

> The word "desire" means *"to sire"* or *"to father."*
> In other words, that strong impulse to achieve something is actually the "something" already in you, seeking to come out!

When you *"sire"* a horse — you have *fathered* it. So the *desire* of Father God is to see the life of His Son be planted in your life, so that you may grow up into an oak tree of righteousness!

> *"Hope deferred makes the heart sick, but when the* **desire** *comes, it is a Tree of Life."* (Proverbs 13:12)

The Devil also has much *desire* for your life!

> *"And the Lord said, Simon, Simon, behold, Satan hath **desired** to have you, that he may sift you as wheat."* (Luke 22:31)

When you come under a deep compulsion of lust, which Father do you think is trying to *sire* (father it, birth it) that within you?

The book of James says that when **desire** is *conceived* — it gives birth to sin, and when sin comes to maturity — it brings forth death! Even after we become Christians, we are constantly at war with two laws at work in our body – like Paul says in the book of Romans.

> *"I find then a law, that evil is present with me, the one who wills to do good. For I delight in the law of God according to the inward man. But I see another law in my members, warring against the law of my mind, and bringing me into captivity to the law of sin which is in my members. O wretched man that I am! Who will deliver me from this body of death? I thank God—through Jesus Christ our Lord!" So then, with the mind I myself serve the law of God, but with the flesh the law of sin.*
> *(Romans 7:21-25)*

You cannot serve two Masters. When we invite Jesus into our hearts, the **Desire** *of the Nations* brings His Holy Presence (Spirit) to come and live within us. He begins the process of drawing us away from carnal living (and thinking) and leads us into Truth about sin, exposing the lies of the Devil we have believed (and served), and begins the process of freeing us to live Godly lives in Jesus! It was for that very freedom that Christ came to set us free from that yoke of slavery to our sin nature. Praise the Lord Jesus Christ!

"Jesus answered them, "Most assuredly, I say to you,
whoever commits sin is a slave of sin. And a slave does not
abide in the house forever, but a son abides forever. Therefore if
the Son makes you free, you shall be free indeed." (John 8:34-36)

Even after we begin to grow in our Christian faith (walk), and start to experience a victorious lifestyle, where we are gaining more and more victory over the old nature within us, our hearts still need a deep purifying work to purge out the vile impurities. It is a long and difficult process, but the rewards are priceless. It is the road to Christlikeness in us – which is the ultimate *desire* of Father God!

During the process, we constantly think we are farther along than we really are. Our hearts are far more evil and deceptive than we ever could have imagined.

"The heart is deceitful above all things, and desperately
wicked; who can know it?" (Jeremiah 17:9)

In the book of Revelation, Jesus sent His Testimony to seven churches (cities). The first six churches He commended for their works, although He confronted certain issues within each of them. The Lord also offered incredible promises to them if they would obey His mandates.

But to the seventh one, the Church at Laodicea, the Lord offered no commendation at all. Laodicea was a wealthy and industrious city, and the Church there had grown lukewarm. They had allowed the deceitfulness of riches and other *desires* to choke out the Word within them.

174

The most deceptive thing about their lives (hearts) is that they *truly* believed they were a rich, blessed, and fully sufficient (having need of nothing) Church. The Lord spoke into that Church with a true assessment and reality of their spiritual condition. The Lord also offered them wise counsel…

> *"I counsel you to **buy from Me gold refined in the fire**, that you may be rich; and white garments, that you may be clothed, that the shame of your nakedness may not be revealed; and anoint your eyes with eye salve, that you may see. As many as I love, I rebuke and chasten. Therefore be zealous and repent. Behold, I stand at the door and knock. If anyone hears My voice and opens the door, I will come in to him and dine with him, and he with Me. To him who overcomes I will grant to sit with Me on My throne, as I also overcame and sat down with My Father on His throne!" (Revelation 3:18-21)*

Many scholars believe there is an overlaying prophetic chronology of the letters delivered to the seven Churches in Revelation. Many believe that not only did these letters to the Churches speak truth with "short range prophetic relevance and fulfillment in their day," but also contained "longer range prophetic and symbolic revelation." That the letters depicted the seven Churches of Jesus Christ progressively right up to Laodicea, the seventh and *final* Church letter, which they say speaks of the "last day" Church.

Whether that is true or not – the counsel, and admonition that Jesus Christ gave to the Church at Laodicea is both timeless and relevant to all Christians. We are admonished to "buy Gold from Him… gold that has been tried in the fire! To be clothed in garments of righteousness (His Righteousness), and to receive from the Lord, a healing salve into our eyes – that we may see clearly (and not remain deceived).

To achieve this, the first order of business is to *buy* (purchase) this gold tried in the fire. This means that we must pay the price, or in other words… it will *cost* us!

Embracing the Lord's process to cleanse and purify us in His Holy Fire, is similar to the process of bringing forth pure gold! To those who yield to the process, they will experience glorious transformation into Christ-like character, and end up fulfilling the ultimate intentions (**desire**) God has for their lives!

Throughout the Bible, there is a constant reference to the refinement of gold and silver in regard to the ways the Lord purifies our hearts.

When the Lord first fills our hearts, He becomes enthroned in the areas of our heart where we have surrendered Lordship to Him. But everyone comes to the Lord *conditionally* at first, whether they realize it or not. We all have areas of hardness of heart, and areas of selfishness we aren't ready to completely give up just yet, and that is where the Lord diligently goes to work. The process is continual and seems like it never stops.

The Lord has to break up the hard areas in our hearts and our will. It's like the breaking up of hard rock (ore) to get down to the precious gold and silver within those areas. The Lord is a Master Miner and has an incredible number of tools (ways) to accomplish this. The treasure is within us – and God delights in unearthing it in our lives.

> "For it is God who commanded light to shine out of darkness, who has **shone in our hearts** to give the light of the knowledge of the Glory of God in the face of Jesus Christ. **But we have this treasure in earthen vessels**, that the excellence of the power may be of God and not of us." (2 Corinthians 4:6, 7)

His Word is like a fire shut up in our bones (even down to the very marrow of our bones), and that Word will not return void but will accomplish all He has sent it to do. His Word will test us, and try us, and purify us. It is mighty powerful!

> *"For the Word of God is **living and powerful**, and sharper than any two-edged sword, <u>piercing even to the division of soul and spirit, and of joints and marrow</u>, and is a discerner of the <u>thoughts and intents of the heart</u>."* (Hebrews 4:12)

So, the beginning of the breaking up of the hardness in our hearts comes through the Word (The Bible) and the Spirit (the Holy Spirit – the Spirit of Truth).

> *"Is not My Word like a fire?" says the* LORD*, and like a* **hammer that breaks the rock in pieces?"** *(Jeremiah 23:29)*

The Lord knows how to *pulverize* the hard rock areas in our heart, just like a miner does for gold, in order to reach the precious metals that are deeply contained within us. Then His process to bring forth pure gold and silver continues…

Once the Lord brings us into a place of brokenness, He still has to refine the precious gold and silver to *separate* it from all the impurities (evil and wickedness in our hearts) and alloys (worldly values and desires). The Lord places all the crumbled ore into the crucible, and turns up the heat to the necessary temperature that will cause the *dross* to rise to the top so the Lord can skim it off and dispose of it – because it's worthless!

> **"Take away the dross from silver,** *and it will go to the silversmith for jewelry."* (Proverbs 25:4)

The Lord knows how to "smith" us properly! To bring forth the purest gold and silver from our hearts, the Lord turns the heat up even higher, and repeats the process seven times! Each time the temperature is slightly hotter, causing even more dross to surface at each level. Seven is the number of perfection! His Word and ways have done the job!

> *"The Words of the LORD are pure words, like silver tried in the furnace of earth, **purified seven times**." (Psalms 12:6)*

The Word didn't need purifying, the earth (our humanity) did! We get tempered over time. Does not a righteous man fall **seven times**!

This process can only come through severe testing and trials in our life. There is no short–cut to this development. But what it produces in us far outweighs the extreme difficulties we experience while going through it.

> *"The refining pot is for silver and the furnace for gold, But the LORD **tests the hearts**." (Proverbs 17:3)*

> *"But He knows the way that I take; when He has tested me, **I shall come forth as gold**." (Job 23:10)*

The beauty of this refinement process is that it produces Godly character in us, humility, and Christlikeness for others to see. There is nothing more precious than when our Lord looks in the crucible of our lives and sees such the purely refined gold - that He sees a clear reflection of Himself in us! How precious!

Malachi 3:2

THE REFINER'S FIRE!

CHAPTER FOURTEEN
A SEA OF GLASS

Chapter Fourteen
A Sea Of Glass

The greatest of all God's creation is humankind. That God would take man from the dust of the earth and then *breathe* into his nostril's the breath of life, until man became a *living* soul! An even greater cause to marvel at this is that prior to creating man, the Godhead, in perfect agreement together, expressed the intention of Their heart in the matter:

> *"Then God said, "Let **Us** make man in **Our** image, according to **Our** likeness; let them have dominion over the fish of the sea, over the birds of the air, and over the cattle, over all the earth and over every creeping thing that creeps on the earth." So God created man in His own image; in the image of God He created him; male and female He created them." (Genesis 1:26, 27)*

With superior, intelligent design and purpose, God created man. The word *breathed* used in Genesis speaks as one *blowing on a fire...* Like the workings of a blacksmith, God "smithed" man with the ability to think, to work, and to worship.

> *"Behold, I have created the blacksmith who blows the coals in the fire, Who brings forth an instrument for his work." (Isaiah 54:16)*

But the mind of man is not the pinnacle of his nature. Far higher, is the spirit of a man, that was created to engage the Spirit of God, in daily, *living* communion and worship – this is the Divine nature that God intended for man to live in. Divine union and harmony with Him!

After the fall, the heart of man, in guilt and shame, wandered away from God, and the work of man became toil, the instinctive worship of a man sought mostly his own pleasure.

The first place we see the English word "Worship" used in the Old Testament is Genesis 22 where Abraham tells his servants that he is going to take his son Isaac and go yonder to *worship* (although the word is used twice before that instance with reference to bowing down).

The plan of God since the fall was to bring man back into worship with His Creator.

We see the Lord continue to carry out His powerful plan by delivering His people out of the House of Bondage in Egypt so they may come to His Holy mountain to *worship* Him.

At the giving of the 10 Commandments on Mt. Sinai, the first three Commandments of God had to do with *worship* and honor to the Lord. As we previously discovered, it was Jesus, the great I AM speaking in Exodus 20 "*I AM the Lord your God.*"

1. You shall have *no* other gods before Me.
2. You shall *not* make idols.
3. You shall *not* take the name of the LORD your God in vain.

While Moses is receiving these Commandments atop the mountain, the people are down below in jubilant praise and dance, *worshipping* a golden calf! When Moses comes down and sees this, he is angered and smashes the two Tablets of Testimony, which had been written by the finger of God!

Then Moses confronts the people and challenges them to return unto the Lord. At the entrance of the camp Moses shouts:

"Whoever is on the LORD's side—come to me!" (Exodus 32:26)

Sadly that day, only the Tribe of Levi came out from among all the tribes of Israel and crossed over to the Lord's side. They ended up becoming the *priestly* tribe unto the Lord.

From that time on, mankind went back and forth between seeking out the true and living God, while also worshipping idols and strange gods of every kind.

The Lord continually pursued His people through the years, longing to bring them back into covenant relationship with Him, for the Lord deeply loved them.

But man chose to continually go his own way. The Bible tells us every man has gone astray – each his own way!

> *"All we like sheep have gone astray; we have turned,*
> *everyone, to his own way..." (Isaiah 53:6)*

The heart of man got darker and darker, in desperate need of a Saviour who could deliver man from a fallen and carnal nature. For God knew the condition of men's hearts and was working out His marvelous plan to give man a new heart!

> *"For I will set My eyes on them for good, and I will bring*
> *them back to this land; I will build them and not pull*
> *them down, and I will plant them and not pluck them up.*
> *Then **I will give them a heart to know Me**, that I am the LORD;*
> *and they shall be My people, and I will be their God, for they*
> *shall return to Me with their whole heart." (Jeremiah 24:6, 7)*

> ***"I will give you a new heart and put a new spirit** within you;*
> *I will take the heart of stone out of your flesh and give you a heart*
> *of flesh. I will put My Spirit within you and cause you to walk*

in My statutes, and you will keep My judgments and do them.
Then you shall dwell in the land that I gave to your fathers; you
shall be My people, and I will be your God." (Ezekiel 36:26-28)

The Prophet Isaiah accurately foretold about the coming Saviour of the world – and what His death would accomplish.

Isaiah said that the coming Saviour, Jesus the Christ (Messiah) had no form (outer beauty) or comeliness (splendor) that men would be drawn to Him by. Isaiah said He would be despised and rejected and become a man of sorrows, well acquainted with grief, and that man would hide their faces from Him.

The prophet went on to say that this Saviour would bear *our* griefs, and carry *our* sorrows, that He would be wounded for *our* transgressions and bruised for *our* iniquities. This Saviour would be chastised to gain *us* peace and whipped to purchase *our* healing, in order to give *us* new life, and freedom, as well as be restored to a right relationship (Covenant) with God.

Jesus Christ died the death that <u>we</u> all deserved, He took our place on the cross, and bore a sentence of capital punishment on our behalf…and He did it willingly!

At His death, the veil was instantly torn. At His resurrection, the New Testament (Will) of God was enacted, and Jesus became the Firstborn among many brethren.

About a week after His ascension into Heaven, the outpouring of the Holy Spirit fell in an upper room during Pentecost and it conceived, and brought forth the New Testament Church!

The moment man began to experience the Baptism of the Holy Spirit or the *indwelling* of the Holy Spirit, was one of the most important events in human history! For man was not only reconciled back to God, but man *literally* became the habitation of the living, Holy God! Man became the Temple of God!

But that was only the beginning of God's marvelous plan for man! The Bible tells us that once Jesus ascended into Heaven, that He gave precious gifts to the Church in the form of ordained Apostles, Prophets, Pastors, Teachers and Evangelists, to help strengthen the Church and equip the Church and its members for the work of the ministry.

This Church that Jesus purchased with His own blood was endowed with incredible blessings and access to God and His power! The early Church quickly discovered just how powerful the blood of Jesus was. His blood not only cleansed us, but it also sanctified us, and then gave access to pass through the veil, enabling us to come before the very Throne of Almighty God!

> *"Therefore, brethren, having boldness to enter the Holiest by the blood of Jesus, by a new and living way which He consecrated for us, through the veil, that is, His flesh, and having a High Priest over the house of God, let us draw near with a true heart in full assurance of faith, having our hearts sprinkled from an evil conscience and our bodies washed with pure water." (Hebrews 10:19-22)*

Think of it... We have been given 24–hour access to come before the Throne of God! In the Old Testament, only one person in the entire nation of Israel could experience this – and he had to be a High Priest! Even then the High Priest could only pass through the veil only one day a year, on the Day of Atonement. What awesome blessings we have received!

But God's incredible plan doesn't even stop there either! God's will wasn't for us to just occasionally visit there – but to live there – in His Presence. The New Testament assures us:

*"In Him you were also circumcised with the circumcision made without hands, by putting off the body of the sins of the flesh, by the circumcision of Christ, **buried with Him in baptism, in which you also were raised with Him** through faith in the working of God, who raised Him from the dead."* (Colossians 2:11, 12)

*But God, who is rich in mercy, because of His great love with which He loved us, even when we were dead in trespasses, **made us alive together with Christ (by grace you have been saved), and raised us up together, and <u>made us sit together in the heavenly places in Christ Jesus</u>**...*" (Ephesians 2:4-6)

Wow! This is such a fantastic plan of God! To as many as received God, He gave them the right (by adoption) to become the sons of God, giving us access to come and live spiritually in His Heavenly home with Him! And not just live there, like an immigrant – His country (Heaven) became *our* country too!

*"**For our citizenship is <u>in Heaven</u>**, from which we also eagerly wait for the Savior, the Lord Jesus Christ, who will transform our lowly body that it may be conformed to His glorious body, according to the working by which He is able even to subdue all things to Himself."* (Philippians 3:20)

*I have given them Your word; and the world has hated them because **they are not of the world**, just as I am not of the world. I do not pray that You should take them out of the world, but that You should keep them from the evil one. **They are not of the world**, just as I am not of the world. Sanctify them by Your Truth. Your Word is Truth."* (John 17:14-17)

We are in the world – but not of the world! Our spirit, made alive from dead works by the regeneration work of the Holy Spirit has made us *new* creatures in Christ Jesus, and we are <u>now</u> seated with our King, Jesus Christ in Heavenly places!

If that were not enough, God has also lavished upon us, additional blessings to fullest possible measure:

> *"Blessed be the God and Father of our Lord Jesus Christ,*
> **who has blessed us with <u>every</u> spiritual blessing in the**
> **heavenly places in Christ**, *just as He chose us in Him*
> *before the foundation of the world, that we should be holy*
> *and without blame before Him in love, having predestined*
> *us to adoption as sons by Jesus Christ to Himself, according to*
> *the good pleasure of His will, to the praise of the glory of His grace,*
> *by which He made us accepted in the Beloved." (Ephesians 1:3-6)*

Therein lies an even greater mystery! God having done all of this, didn't just plan for us to be spectators in that Heavenly place... the Throne Room of God! We not only have a place there but far more *purpose* and *function* there as well!

We were created by God for worship! It is inherent in man to worship, whether it be God or something else... During His earthly ministry, Jesus had a profound encounter with a Samaritan woman by a well. What Jesus spoke to her gave us all - beautiful insight into the heart and desire of Father God:

> *"Jesus said to her, "Woman, believe Me, the hour is coming*
> *when you will neither on this mountain, nor in Jerusalem,*
> *worship the Father. You worship what you do not know; we*
> *know what we worship, for salvation is of the Jews. But the*
> *hour is coming, and now is, when the **true worshipers will***
> ***worship the Father in Spirit and Truth**; for the Father is*
> *<u>seeking such to worship Him</u>. God is Spirit, and those who*

worship Him must worship in Spirit and Truth." The woman said
to Him, "I know that Messiah is coming" (who is called Christ).
"When He comes, He will tell us all things. Jesus said to her,
*"I who speak to you – **I AM** HE (ego eimi)." (John 4:21-26*

The Father is longing for us to be filled with His Holy **Spirit**, and to worship Him in **Truth**, which is being in Christ, for Jesus is the Way, the **Truth**, and the Life! When we enter His gates (coming before His Throne), we begin to become cognizant that we entered a place of eternal *reality* and Glory! We stepped into an environment of continual worship – it never ceases there!

Everything in Heaven is focused on the Glorious God. The Seraphim and Cherubim Angels, the 24 Elders, the 4 Living Creatures, myriads upon myriads of other angels, the Cloud of Witnesses, the Saints of God who have gone on before us, and the Body of Christ in Spirit, worshipping Truth Himself!

Waves after waves of Glory emanate from the Throne and all the inhabitants in Heaven are engulfed in new, unfolding revelations of His Holiness, Worthiness, Glory, and Power. They constantly cast down their crowns and fall before Him in unending fascination and utter ecstatic praise and worship!

We have both honor and privilege to join the processions of Heaven that go before the Throne. We must learn how to move into deeper and deeper realms of unfolding Glory and Revelation of our God and King! It is the Spirit of God, that is… the Spirit of Truth, that not only testifies of Jesus, but ignites our spirit man into deep worship, understanding, and beholding God! It's God's Spirit that causes praise to arise!

"I will greatly rejoice in the LORD, my soul shall be joyful
in my God; for He has clothed me with the garments of
salvation, He has covered me with the robe of righteousness,

188

*As a bridegroom decks himself with ornaments, and as a
bride adorns herself with her jewels. For as the earth brings
forth its bud, as the garden causes the things that are sown in
it to spring forth, so the Lord GOD will cause **righteousness and
praise to spring forth before all the nations.**" (Isaiah 61:10, 11)*

*"Among the gods there is none like You, O Lord; nor
are there any works like Your works. **All nations whom
You have made shall come and worship before You, O Lord,**
And shall glorify Your name. for You are great, and do
wondrous things; You alone are God." (Psalm 86:8-10)*

As John the Beloved is taken through a door into the Throne
Room of Heaven, he sees the most amazing worship unto the
King Eternal. He is amazed at the unending Glory and Majesty
of God, and everything and everyone there is transfixed upon
God – and God alone! Then John said he saw a crystal river:

*"Immediately I was in the Spirit; and behold, a
Throne set in Heaven, and One sat on the Throne.*

*Before the Throne there was a sea of glass,
like crystal." (Revelation 4:2,6)*

This sea of glass is a company of ardent worshippers before
God, burning in zeal, and abandonment in worship unto their
God. They are called the *laid–down lovers* of God, who are so in
love with Jesus, they have laid down their own lives, their own
wills, and have embraced the fiery work of God in their lives in
purifying, cleansing, and being *jeweled* into precious living
stones with radiant fire! Like the brilliance of the world's most
perfectly cut diamond – the "Hearts On Fire" Diamond:

189

Hearts On Fire diamonds have a perfect ring of eight hearts on the bottom and a perfectly formed, symmetrical Fireburst® on the top that outshines every other diamond!

As *"Light"* enters the diamond, it descends downward into the pavilion. A standard diamond with an inferior cut leaks light from the bottom and sides. Too deep or too shallow a cut, and the light that gives a diamond its brilliance is lost. However, because of its perfectly symmetrical cut and increased surface area, a "Hearts On Fire" Diamond captures that light and reflects it from the top, creating maximum brilliance and fire!

The amazing thing about this sea of glass is that John said that it was *mingled* with fire!

> *"And I saw something like a **sea of glass mingled with fire**, and those who have the victory over the beast, over his image and over his mark and over the number of his name, standing on the sea of glass, having harps of God. They sing the song of Moses, the servant of God, and the song of the Lamb, saying:*
>
> *"Great and marvelous are Your works, Lord God Almighty! Just and true are Your ways, O King of the saints! Who shall not fear You, O Lord, and glorify Your name? For You alone are holy. For all nations shall come and worship before You, For Your judgments have been manifested."*
> *(Revelation 15:2-4)*

The fiery worshippers of God in this sea of glass have overcome self, the world, the beast and everything else. They kept the Testimony of Jesus and endured their lives being purified in the crucible! The dross was burned out of their lives through Holy Fire, and they were given the greatest honor – to stand before the King of Fire Himself, and sing the Song of Moses and the Song of the Lamb, in the highest echelons of worship one could ever offer unto the Lord!

Don't you want to be in that company too? Let the Holy Fire of God have its full way with you to become as translucent fire!

Sea of Glass (Rev 4:6 & 15:2)

A SEA OF FIERY WORSHIPPERS!

A COMPANY OF OVERCOMERS!

CHAPTER FIFTEEN
SEVEN LAMPS OF FIRE

Chapter Fifteen
Seven Lamps Of Fire

About 700 years before the birth of Christ, the Prophet Isaiah had prophesied a series of stunning revelations concerning the coming Messiah. Isaiah reveals this One would be a ruler:

> *"For unto us a Child is born, unto us a Son is given; and the **government** will be upon His shoulder..." (Isaiah 9:6)*

In the same scripture, Isaiah continues to detail the awesome attributes of this coming King, and his prophecies gave us the clearest vision and portrayal of Christ in the Old Testament!

> *"...And His name will be called **Wonderful, Counselor, Mighty God, Everlasting Father, Prince of Peace." (Isaiah 9:6)***

A. **Wonderful.** Extraordinary, miraculous, distinguished.
B. **Counselor.** Consult, advise, resolve, guide, command.
C. **Mighty God.** Strong, powerful, warrior, champion, hero, mighty in battle, the true God.
D. **Everlasting Father.** From eternity, continuing forever, purpose, family, head or founder of the household.
E. **Prince of Peace.** Completeness, soundness, welfare, peace, health, prosperity, relationship as in covenant.

Isaiah declared the lineage of this Messiah would come forth as a rod (branch) out of Jesse, down through the house of David. Jesus Christ is the *Righteous Branch*, from the *Root of David*.

> *"Behold, the days are coming," says the* LORD, *that I will raise to David a **Branch of Righteousness; A King** shall reign and prosper, and execute judgment and righteousness in the earth." (Jeremiah 23:5)*

*"...Behold, the Lion of the tribe of Judah, the **Root of David**, has prevailed to open the scroll and to loose its seven seals." (Revelation 5:5)*

Isaiah goes on to release an incredible revelatory view into this promised King. He declares that the Sevenfold Spirit of God would rest on Him – which was the first revelation of Sevenfold Spirit of God in the Bible. What exactly is the Sevenfold Spirit of God? A very good question... With an even more amazing answer!

First and foremost, these prophecies refer to the coming Messiah. The word Messiah in Hebrew is *mashiyach*, and it means "Anointed." The Anointed One has the full weight of The Holy Spirit *resting* upon Him. The Holy Spirit is the Sevenfold Spirit of God!

The Sevenfold Spirit of God is not seven Holy Spirits; He is one Holy Spirit with a *sevenfold nature*. Seven is the number of perfection and completeness. The sevenfold manifestations in the *Presence* of Holy Spirit represent the fullness of His attributes and characteristics in the Godhead, which better said is the sevenfold *endowments* of God!

The Spirit of the Lord

The Spirit that would rest upon the Messiah was the Holy Spirit, that is, the 3rd Person of the Godhead, the Trinity. Remember that Jesus emptied Himself of all privilege of Deity, considering equality with God, not something He would take ahold, even though He is the 2nd person of the Godhead! (He refused executive privilege and power - according to the Bible).

Everything Jesus did while in His earthly ministry, He did as 100% man, completely reliant on the power of the Holy Spirit!

196

"...being in the form of God, did not consider it robbery to be equal with God, but made Himself of no reputation, taking the form of a bondservant, and coming in the __likeness of men__." (Philippians 2:6, 7)

Since the Holy Spirit is Omniscience, meaning as God, He knows *everything* there is to know. There is nothing that the Holy Spirit doesn't know...

"But God has revealed them to us through His Spirit. For the Spirit searches all things, yes, <u>the deep things of God</u>. For what man knows the things of a man except the spirit of the man which is in him? Even so **no one knows the things of God except the Spirit of God**. *Now we have received, not the spirit of the world, but the Spirit who is from God, that we might know the things that have been freely given to us by God." (1 Corinthians 2:10-12)*

The sevenfold Spirit of God anointed Jesus with the perfect mind of God. That is how He continually walked in the perfect will of God, and only did what He saw the Father doing (as was revealed by the Holy Spirit), and only spoke what He heard the Father speaking – again, by the illumination of the Holy Spirit! The Bible says we too can have the mind of the Spirit, that is, the mind of Christ. Read 1 Corinthians 2:16.

The Spirit of Wisdom

Wisdom is the genius of God at work. It is operating in the highest thoughts of God – which are perfect. Just look at what the Word of God says about Wisdom:

I, Wisdom was established before the beginning, from everlasting. Before fountains of water, mountains and hills were created, I was brought forth. When God prepared the heavens, I was there. When He marked out the boundaries of the earth, I was there, as a *master craftsmen*.

I dwell with all prudence and find out knowledge and discretion. To have the fear of the Lord is beginning of my path. Counsel is mine, and sound wisdom. I am understanding; I have strength. By me King's reign and Rulers decree justice. By me Prince's rule, and Nobles. I love those that love me.

Riches and honor are with me, enduring riches and righteousness. My fruit is better than gold, yes, than even fine gold. My revenue is far better than choice silver. I traverse the ways of righteousness. Blessed are those who keep my ways!

I, Wisdom, am the mind of God, yes, the mind of the Spirit, even the mind of Christ! Blessed is the man who listens to me, watches for me daily at the gates, waiting at the posts of my doors. Whoever finds me, finds life, and obtains Favor from the Lord, but he who sins against me, wrongs his own soul, and all those who hate me, love death.

The Spirit of Understanding

It is the power of the Holy Spirit operating within us to differentiate between varying things, with perception and discernment.

It empowers you to root out what is of God and what is of man, that is, what is of the Spirit and what is of the soul, or even the flesh. It is to us, the endowment of comprehension of the Word of God! It brings illumination to the Scriptures!

It is like having x-ray vision into a matter, to see clearly, the preference of God, according to His Word, and His principles.

The Bible says:

> "...And in all your getting, **get understanding**. Exalt her,
> and she will promote you; she will bring you honor, when you
> embrace her. She will place on your head an ornament of grace;
> A **crown of glory** she will deliver to you." (Proverbs 4:7-9)

The Spirit of Counsel

The beautiful Spirit of Counsel implants in us the mind of God in such a way that He advises us, instructs us, and acts as an expert consultant.

It is the very power of the Holy Spirit in receiving strategies from God, and the Divine Blueprints of Heaven in situations, so that we operate and flow in harmony with God!

The Spirit of Counsel is the Divine Guidance of God. The Lord provides counsel in making the best decisions, and taking the best path – especially when there might be more than one path before you!

> "I will instruct you and teach you in the way you
> should go; I will guide you with My eye." (Psalm 32:8)

The Lord declares that His ways are higher than our ways, and His thoughts are higher than our thoughts. The Spirit of Counsel is reaching up to receive His preferred thoughts, way and methods, instead of trying to rely on our own efforts.

We have access to this precious power, twenty-four hours a day, because the Holy Spirit lives within us, which is the Spirit of Christ, and Jesus is both by name and in function – The *Wonderful Counselor*! All the treasure of Wisdom and Knowledge are in Christ Jesus! Read Colossians 2:3.

The Spirit of Might

We need the strength and power of God manifesting in every area of our lives and ministry. The Spirit of Might is the explosive power of God released in us and around us to accomplish the very things ordained of God that we might fulfill His will and purpose in the earth! It is ill–advised to try and confront any challenge or battle without the power and strength of the Might of God. He is a *Mighty God*!

When you align yourself with the will and purpose of God in any difficulty, you have access to the release of God's power and strength. Quit trying to conquer the situations yourself! Call on the *Mighty One* to move on your behalf, and the Lord will move *mightily* according to His plans and timetables. Your job is to trust Him to prevail in the when, and way He chooses.

You just need to rest – in faith… The Lord says "I'll do the *heavy lifting* and you do the *rest*!

> *"Lift up your heads, O you gates! And be lifted up,*
> *you everlasting doors! And the King of glory shall come*
> *in. Who is this King of Glory? The LORD **strong and mighty**,*
> *The LORD **mighty in battle**." (Psalm 24:7, 8)*

The Spirit of Knowledge

The Spirit of Knowledge is possessing (harboring) keen insights that do not just come from books or study, but through life experience in your spiritual journey following Christ, through the leading of the Holy Spirit.

The Spirit of Knowledge is the Spirit of Truth at work in our lives. It is not having "head knowledge" but rather "heart knowledge" as the Spirit of Knowledge (Truth) leads us into all

Truth. We receive these precious revelations through intimate, life–changing encounters – experientially, by illumination!

The path towards coming to maturity in God is powered by the Spirit of Knowledge. We learn how to avoid mistakes, pitfalls, and instead of continually going *around* the mountain – we learn how to go *up* the mountain!

> *"The tongue of the wise uses **knowledge** rightly, but the mouth of fools pours forth foolishness." (Proverbs 15:2)*

> *"The heart of the prudent acquires **knowledge**, and the ear of the wise seeks **knowledge**." (Proverbs 18:15)*

The Bible says that God's people are destroyed for *lack of knowledge*. This does not mean a *lack of information*.

> *"My people are destroyed for lack of **knowledge**. Because you have rejected **knowledge**." (Hosea 4:6)*

The Hebrew word used there is *da`ath* and it means:

A. Perception, discernment, understanding, wisdom.

In its purest sense, the Spirit of Knowledge is an office work (endowment and operation) of the Holy Spirit bringing you into a deepening and intimate knowledge of *knowing* God, and His ways. We must learn (knowledge) to walk in His ways!

When Paul said, "Oh that I may *know* Him, and the power of His resurrection," that word *know* was the exact same word Mary, the Mother of Jesus used when she told the Angel, "How can this be (that I am pregnant) since I *know* no man?"

It speaks of true intimacy with God.

The Spirit of the Fear of the Lord

This is probably the most misunderstood portion of the Sevenfold Spirit. The Spirit of the Fear of the Lord is a deep work in the heart of man by the Holy Spirit. It opens up the heart to behold God as He really is!

It produces a true, reverential awe, marvel, respect and honor of God as the deepening revelation of His Majesty, Kingship, Glory, Authority, Power, Holiness and Worthiness begin to flood our dark and weak hearts. It breaks down our earlier definitions and concepts of God, allowing us to see Him with clearer Greatness. It leaves a person stunned, without words!

Experiencing God's Presence in the Spirit of the Fear of the Lord causes us to long even more for Him, to draw nearer, and to become much more willing to allow a change in our lives and our hearts. We begin to recognize the areas of our lives that are not fully submitted to Him and are deeply stirred within our hearts to make an effort to bring those areas under His Lordship, bringing us into more unity with God!

> *"Teach me Your way, O LORD; I will walk in Your truth;*
> ***Unite*** *my heart to fear Your name." (Psalm 86:11)*

Many Christians have been held captive by a demonic type of "the fear of God," as they see Him as an angry God who is greatly displeased with them. Their fear is always measured by their performance.

The Bible says that the *perfect love* of God casts out this type of fear because it always has to do with punishment – because in their minds – they never measure up and either believe (or expect) to be punished by God.

God is Love! He wants us to see the hope of our calling, the riches of His Glory, and to experience the greatness of His power working in us! He is an Awesome God! He is *terrible* in the sense of His awesome Holiness & Power! Remember that the very foundation of the Throne of God is Righteousness and Justice! He executes justice in the Nations, and vengeance is His against His enemies!

But we who abide in the shelter of His wings, and under His feathers in the secret place – that is the Pavilion of God, are safe from the *terror of the Lord* even though:

> *"It is a fearful thing to fall into the hands of the living God."*
> (Hebrew 10:31)

Our *first* insights into the Sevenfold Spirit of God from the Bible come at the building of the Tabernacle of Moses. Moses is instructed by God to build each part of the Tabernacle *exactly* according to the pattern of Heaven.

One of the pieces of the Tabernacle was the seven–branched Menorah, which was to remain in the Tabernacle and to remain *burning* at all times. The Menorah was seven–lamps upon one lampstand, made of pure gold. It was clearly served both prophetic and symbolic imagery of the Sevenfold Spirit of God.

We can see even more clarity from the Book of Zechariah concerning the amazing Seven–fold Lamp, which represents the Sevenfold Spirit of God. Zechariah has a vision of a Golden Lampstand with seven lamps. He asks the Angel who awakened him what the meaning of the seven lamps was. The Angel said to him:

"This is the word of the LORD to Zerubbabel:
'Not by might nor by power, but by My Spirit,'
Says the LORD of hosts. 'Who are you, O great mountain?
Before Zerubbabel you shall become a plain!
And he shall bring forth the capstone
With shouts of 'Grace, grace to it!''"

Moreover, the word of the LORD came to me, saying:

"The hands of Zerubbabel Have laid the foundation of
this temple; his hands shall also finish it. Then you will know
that the LORD of hosts has sent Me to you. For who has despised
the day of small things? For these seven rejoice to see the plumb line
in the hand of Zerubbabel. **They are the eyes of the LORD**, *which*
scan to and fro throughout the whole earth." (Zechariah 4:6-10)

Not by might (human strength), nor by power (armies), but by My Spirit saith the Lord! These Scriptures are very significant!

The Sevenfold Spirit of God was upon Jesus the entire time of His earthly ministry. One could argue that it could have been operating in His life long before His Baptism in the Holy Spirit at the Jordan, for we see Jesus – at 12 years old, astounding the Pharisees & Sadducees with both His knowledge and His understanding of Scripture - for someone of His age at the time.

We understand now the Sevenfold *nature* or endowments of the Holy Spirit. They are available to the New Testament believer and followers of Christ. That is awesome! But let's take an even *closer* look at the Sevenfold Spirit of God!

For that, we will need to go to the snapshot of the Throne of God that John, the Disciple of Jesus provided us in the opening chapters of the Book of Revelation…

As John is taken up into Heaven through a door, he sees the very Throne of God is all its Glory and splendor. John saw One sitting on the Throne, who looked like a jasper and sardius stone, covered by a rainbow around the Throne, with a sight like unto an emerald.

John saw the Sevenfold Spirit of God! What did it look like? John said he saw Seven Lamps of **Burning Fire**! The Greek Word for lamps here is *lampas* meaning a *torch*, or *lamp* whose flame is fed with oil.

As it was revealed in the fourth chapter of Zechariah, that the Sevenfold Lamp represented **the eyes of the Lord** looking out upon all of the earth, the Book of Revelation gives us an even clearer *revelation* into the mystery of the Sevenfold Spirit of God and how it operates in and through Jesus Christ!

> *"And out of the throne proceeded lightnings and thunderings and there were **seven lamps of fire burning** before the Throne, which are the seven Spirits of God." (Revelation 4:5)*

> *And I looked, and behold, in the midst of the Throne and of the four living creatures, and in the midst of the elders, **stood a Lamb as though it had been slain, having <u>seven horns</u> and <u>seven eyes</u>, which are the seven Spirits of God sent out into all the earth."*** (Revelation 5:6)*

This is the most incredible glimpse into our Lord Jesus Christ! There He is in Heaven, in perfect alignment and agreement with His Father, as They are also in perfect synchronicity with the Sevenfold Spirit (The Holy Spirit).

The Lord is looking out to and fro throughout all the earth with seven eyes, speaking of complete union and partnership of the Holy Spirit and His Sevenfold Divine nature – the perfect Mind

205

of God, so that in everything Jesus sees the world from a perfect view and with perfect understanding!

But the Scripture also depicts Jesus not only with seven eyes but with seven horns too! The seven horns represent POWER!

Thus Jesus is ruling, and reigning in perfect vision for His eyes see all across the entire earth, He makes perfect judgments because He has the full Mind of God, through the seven endowments of the Holy Spirit and He administrates *dunamis* power over what He sees and knows as He rules through the seven horns of power of the Holy Spirit!

Is this not the clearest understanding of the Trinity of God at work? The "three-in-one" God who is OMNIPRESENT (He is everywhere at the same time), OMNISCIENCE (He is the All–Knowing God), OMNIPOTENT (He is the All–Powerful God)!

The Sevenfold Spirit of God is akin to burning, Holy Fire! The fire from those lamps should burn within us – with wisdom and power - as it does in Christ Jesus! It is available to us!

The Sevenfold Spirit can bring us the Mind of God with multiple manifestations of superior insights, wisdom, revelation, strategy and so much more! It can bring transformation (Literally *transfiguration*) to our minds!

> *"I beseech you therefore, brethren, by the mercies of God,*
> *that you present your bodies a living sacrifice, holy, acceptable*
> *to God, which is your reasonable service. And do not be conformed*
> *to this world, but be **transformed** by the **renewing** of your mind, that*
> *you may prove what is that good and acceptable and perfect will of God."*
> *(Romans 12:1, 2)*

The word **transformed** here is *"metamorphoō,"* and it is the same word used for the transfiguration of Christ! The word **renewing** is *anakainōsis* in the Greek and means renovation, complete change for the better – and it is the work of The Holy Spirit! The Sevenfold Spirit of God!

A STUDY IN THE BOOK OF

REVELATION

Seven Lamps of the Menorah   Isaiah 11:2

Each lamp of the menorah represents a ministry of the Holy Spirit

1. *The Spirit of the Lord*
2. *The Spirit of Wisdom*
3. *The Spirit of Understanding*
4. *The Spirit of Counsel*
5. *The Spirit of Might*
6. *The Spirit of Knowledge*
7. *The Spirit of the Fear of the Lord*

THE SEVENFOLD SPIRIT OF GOD

CHAPTER SIXTEEN
THE KING OF
HOLY FIRE

CHAPTER SIXTEEN
THE KING OF
HOLY FIRE

Chapter Sixteen
The King Of Fire

The Lord Jesus Christ is the Eternal Son of Father God, the Great I AM from eternity past, present, and forever! Long before the world was ever created, This King sat enthroned in the semblance of a Lamb. We know this because "The Lamb's Book" of Life was written – *before* the foundation of the earth. Not just *the* Book of Life… but the Lamb's Book of Life! To go it even a step further, the Bible says:

> *"All who dwell on the earth will worship him, whose names*
> *have not been written in the Book of Life of* ***the Lamb - slain***
> ***from the foundation of the world.****" (Revelation 13:8)*

This is clear reference to the imagery of Jesus as the **Lamb of God** – before time. But Jesus was also the King of Heaven before the world began. How do we know this? The Word of God declares that the King-dom (King's Domain) was pre-*pared* for us from eternity past...

> *"Then the King will say to those on His right hand, 'Come,*
> *you blessed of My Father, inherit the Kingdom prepared for*
> *you* ***from the foundation of the world***.*" (Matthew 25:34)*

From eternity past the Kingdom of Heaven was established with us in mind... Knowing full well the impending fall of man, the precious Godhead established an elaborate plan to redeem us from the curse of sin and death, by sending The Lamb King to die in our place.

In order for that to happen, this beautiful Lamb King had to set aside His Crown of Glory and become lower than the Angels and came to us in the form of a man. A humble King, born in a stable. Wisemen brought this King gold, frankincense, and myrrh. We should give Him the same gifts.

A. **Gold**. Allowing Him to purify us and bring forth gold!
B. **Frankincense**. Live a lifestyle of continual intercession!
C. **Myrrh**. Choosing death to self – producing this fragrance!

WHAT WONDROUS LOVE IS THIS

What wondrous love is this, O my soul, O my soul!
What wondrous love is this, O my soul!
What wondrous love is this
That caused the Lord of bliss
To bear the dreadful curse for my soul, for my soul,
To bear the dreadful curse for my soul!

When I was sinking down, sinking down, sinking down,
When I was sinking down, sinking down,
When I was sinking down
Beneath God's righteous frown,
Christ laid aside His crown for my soul for my soul,
Christ laid aside His crown for my soul.

To God and to the Lamb I will sing, I will sing;
To God and to the Lamb I will sing;
To God and to the Lamb,
Who is the great I AM,
While millions join the theme, I will sing, I will sing,
While millions join the theme, I will sing.

And when from death I'm free, I'll sing on, I'll sing on;
And when from death I'm free, I'll sing on.
And when from death I'm free
I'll sing His love for me,
And through eternity I'll sing on, I'll sing on,
And through eternity I'll sing on.

The Bible declares that Jesus was a born King. Those wise men from the east who came to Bethlehem were asking:

*"Where is He who has been **born King of the Jews**? For we have seen His star in the East and have come to worship Him." (Matthew 2:2)*

The people of Israel during the generation of Jesus's earthly ministry lived under the repressive and tyrannical regime of the Romans. They had long awaited the coming of their King.

In their understanding of Scripture, this King would come and rule with a rod of iron. He would vanquish armies, dashing them to pieces like pottery, and rule the whole earth from Zion.

They mistook prophecy that declared the coming rule and reign of Christ Jesus on earth with the mission of Jesus in His earthly ministry of redemption and reconciliation to God.

Once they saw that Jesus truly had supernatural power, they tried to forcibly make Him their earthly King to accomplish the destruction of the Roman Empire.

"Therefore when Jesus perceived that they were about to come and take Him by force to make Him King, He departed again to the mountain by Himself alone." (John 6:15)

But when the time had come for this King to fulfill His ultimate purpose on earth, death upon a cross, He began the journey from Bethany on the backside of the Mt. of Olives. As He came up over the top of the Mt. of Olives, the crowds began to form, hailing Him as their King. They cut down palm branches and laid them before Him as well as their cloaks on the path of the donkey He was riding – all foretold by the Prophet Zechariah:

"Rejoice greatly, O daughter of Zion! Shout, O daughter of Jerusalem!
Behold, your King is coming to you; He is just and having Salvation,
Lowly and riding on a donkey, a colt, the foal of a donkey."
(Zechariah 9:9)

The crowds were jubilant, lifting up high praise and honor to their King, and shouting:

"Hosanna to the Son of David! 'Blessed is He who comes in the name of the LORD! Hosanna in the highest!" *(Matthew 21:9)*

But just days later, this King was betrayed by one of His own disciples and was handed over to the Chief Priests and Pharisees, along with a contingent of troops and officers. An amazing thing happened as they confronted Jesus:

"Jesus therefore, knowing all things that would come upon Him, went forward and said to them, *"Whom are you seeking?"*

They answered Him, *"Jesus of Nazareth."*

Jesus said to them, *"I Am He."* And Judas, who betrayed Him, also stood with them. Now when He said to them,

"I Am He," they drew back and fell to the ground." *(John 18:4-6)*

Jesus declared to them His eternal name **"I AM"** – the power of the truth of that declaration from Jesus of Nazareth was so great and powerful, they all fell to the ground!

After being interrogated by the Chief Priests, they took Him to Pilate, pleading that he put Jesus to death. Pilate told them to take Jesus and judge Him according to their own Law – but they argued it wasn't lawful for them to put Jesus to death.

Pilate then asked Jesus a most powerful question:

"Are You the King of the Jews? (John 18:33)

*Jesus answered, "**You say rightly that I am a King**. For this cause I was born, and for this cause, I have come into the world, that I should bear witness to the Truth. Everyone who is of the Truth hears My voice." (John 18:33)*

Pilate found no cause to sentence Jesus to death, but the people pleaded with him all the more. At this point, Pilate began to refer to Jesus as THE KING OF THE JEWS.

Pilate spoke to the people and said:

*"But you have a custom that I should release someone to you at the Passover. Do you therefore want me to release to you **the King of the Jews**?"*

Then they all cried again, saying, "Not this Man, but Barabbas!" Now Barabbas was a robber." (John 18:39, 40)

Pilate then took Jesus and scourged Him. The Roman soldiers made a crown of twisted thorns to put on his head, and put a purple robe on Him and mocked Him declaring:

"Hail, King of the Jews!"
And they struck Him with their hands.
(John 19:3)

After speaking with Jesus some more, Pilate still wanted to let Him go, but the people insisted if he let Jesus go then Pilate was not a friend of the Caesar because this man Jesus makes Himself out to be a King – against Caesar's laws (sedition).

Pilate brought Jesus down to the judgment seat called *The Pavement,* or in Hebrew *Gabbatha* and declared to the Jews:

"<u>*Behold your King!*</u>" *(John 19:14)*

But they cried out, *"Away with Him, away with Him! Crucify Him!"*

Pilate said to them, "<u>*Shall I crucify your King?*</u>" The Chief Priests answered, *"We have no King but Caesar!"*

At that point, Pilate then authorized Jesus of Nazareth, the KING OF THE JEWS, and the great I AM, to be crucified upon a cross. In parting, Pilate himself made a sign, it was an epitaph to be placed on the head of Jesus (above the cross) that read:

JESUS OF NAZARETH,
KING OF THE JEWS

This epitaph was written in Hebrew, Greek, and Latin for all who were present at the crucifixion to see – clearly defining *who* it was they were crucifying.

When the Chief Priests saw the sign, then went to Pilate and pleaded with him to change the sign to read:

I AM THE KING OF THE JEWS

But Pilate refused them and said what was written is final. That day, on a lonely hill called Mt. Calvary, also known as *Golgotha,* meaning *"The Place of the Skull,"* they crucified the Lord of Glory and not just THE KING OF THE JEWS but:

THE KING OF KINGS

The Apostle Paul, in writing a letter to his son in the faith, Timothy, who was then leading the Church in Ephesus, was reflecting back on his spiritual journey. He gave praise to the Lord Jesus Christ, who Paul recognized had empowered him to preach the Gospel because He had considered Paul faithful.

> *"I was formerly a blasphemer, a persecutor, and an insolent man; but I obtained mercy because I did it ignorantly in unbelief. And the grace of our Lord was exceedingly abundant, with faith and love which are in Christ Jesus. This is a faithful saying and worthy of all acceptance, that Christ Jesus came into the world to save sinners, of whom I am chief. However, for this reason I obtained mercy, that in me, first Jesus Christ might show all longsuffering, as a pattern to those who are going to believe on Him for everlasting life.*

Paul beautifully articulates the unfathomable grace, mercy, and love Jesus has – for even the vilest sinners, of what Paul once was. As Paul is recounting all this, he grasps it from an eternal perspective, realizing that this was all part of the Grand Love Story and plan of God – set into place before the foundation of the world was ever laid.

To think that the everlasting King would give up His Royal Throne, humble Himself to unimaginable depths, and then come to earth to seek and save broken humanity.

> ***Now unto the King eternal***, *immortal, invisible, to God who alone is wise, be honor and glory forever and ever. Amen." (1 Timothy 1:13-17)*

Paul picks up the same track again as he continues to exhort Timothy to righteous living, and honorable service in ministry.

> *"…that you keep this commandment without spot, blameless until our Lord Jesus Christ's appearing, which He will manifest in His own time, He who is the blessed and only **Potentate**, the*

King of kings and Lord of lords, who alone has immortality,
dwelling in unapproachable light, whom no man has seen or
can see, to whom be honor and everlasting power. Amen."
(1 Timothy 6:14-16)

Did you notice the word Potentate? It is Greek for *dynastēs* from which we get the word dynasty. It means royalty, of great authority, a ruler.

This King fulfilled the most difficult mission and ministry on earth. When He ascended back into Heaven, God the Father exalted Him to very highest place. The Bible tells us:

"Therefore God also has highly exalted Him and given Him
the name which is above every name that at the name of
Jesus every knee should bow, of those in Heaven, and of those on
earth, and of those under the earth, and that every tongue should
confess that Jesus Christ is Lord, to the Glory of God the Father."
(Philippians 2:9-11)

The Book of Revelation reveals to us what this King looks like now, as He is seated on the Throne.

"... and in the midst of the seven lampstands One like the Son of Man,
clothed with a garment down to the feet and girded about the chest with a
golden band. His head and hair were white like wool, as white as snow,
*and **His eyes like a flame of fire**; His feet were like fine brass, as if*
***refined in a furnace**, and His voice as the sound of many waters; He had*
in His right hand seven stars, out of His mouth went a sharp two-edged
sword, and His countenance was like the sun shining in its strength."
(Revelation 1:13-16)

"Now I saw heaven opened, and behold, a white horse. And
He who sat on him was called Faithful and True, and in
righteousness He judges and makes war. His eyes were like a
*flame of fire, and on **His head were many crowns**. He had a*

name written that no one knew except Himself. He was clothed with a robe dipped in blood, and His name is called The Word of God. And the armies in Heaven, clothed in fine linen, white and clean, followed Him on white horses. Now out of His mouth goes a sharp sword, that with it He should strike the nations. And He Himself will rule them with a rod of iron. He Himself treads the winepress of the fierceness and wrath of Almighty God. And He has on His robe and on His thigh a name written:

KING OF KINGS AND LORD OF LORDS

This Holy King is emblazed in Fire! Those who saw Him as He is… like Daniel in the Old Testament and John in the New Testament – both declared that He had eyes of burning Fire!

Even the words that proceed forth from this awesome King are as Holy Fire:

> *"His sneezings flash forth light,*
> *And his eyes are like the eyelids of the morning.*
> *Out of his mouth go **burning lights**;*
> ***Sparks of fire shoot out**.*
> *Smoke goes out of his nostrils,*
> *As from a boiling pot and burning rushes.*
> *His breath kindles coals,*
> *And **a flame goes out of his mouth**."*
> *(Job 41:18-21)*

> *"The LORD thundered from Heaven,*
> *And the Most High uttered **His voice**,*
> *Hailstones and **coals of fire**."*
> *(Psalm 18:13)*

The Prophet Isaiah was allowed to look into the times of the end days, and he saw this same King of Fire coming down out of Heaven with great fire:

*"...The hand of the LORD shall be known to His servants,
And His indignation to His enemies. For behold, **the LORD will
come with fire** and with His chariots, like a whirlwind, to render
His anger with fury, and His **rebuke with flames of fire**.
<u>**For by fire and by His sword**</u> the LORD will judge all flesh;
And the slain of the LORD shall be many."* (Isaiah 66:14-16)

John saw the same thing, for the beast (from the Book of
Revelation), the Kings of the earth, and their armies had all
gathered together to make war against the King of Kings...

BEHOLD THE KING OF HOLY FIRE!

CHAPTER SEVENTEEN
A NEW HEAVEN AND
A NEW EARTH

CHAPTER SEVENTEEN
A NEW HEAVEN AND
A NEW EARTH

Chapter Seventeen
A New Heaven And A New Earth

We are at the very end stages of God's marvelous plan being completed. The brilliance of the Lord's glorious wisdom and power are so far beyond our comprehension.

The Lord has executed the most amazing and redemptive recovery of fallen man down through history, that all should stand in awe and wonder!

That God would create man... literally <u>from Himself</u>, with an eternal plan for man to dwell with Him as the family of God *forever* is mind boggling! God had ultimate intentions that He would fully accomplish, and even though he knew that man would sin – it didn't stop Him!

At the fall of man in the garden, the Lord launched His rescue plan for mankind. First, the Lord spoke in prophetic judgment to the serpent telling him that he was cursed and that from the woman there would come forth a "Seed" (Jesus) that would bruise the serpent's head, even though the serpent would bruise his heel. This was the inauguration of God's redemptive plan for man in action!

To Adam, again speaking with prophetic judgment, the Lord says something unusual in His opening statement:

> "**<u>Cursed is the ground for your sake</u>**;
> *In toil you shall eat of it, all the days of your life.*
> *Both thorns and thistles it shall bring forth for you,*
> *And you shall eat the herb of the field. In the sweat of your*
> *face you shall eat bread till you return to the ground,*

For out of it you were taken; for dust you are,
And to dust you shall return." (Genesis 3:17-19)

Little did we know from that Word to Ada that the Lord was saying that the earth itself had now been cursed. But God had a plan for earth too! He makes that very clear down through Scripture. Because it is cursed, the earth will have to eventually be done away with, but in the beautiful plan of God, the Lord is going to make a new earth and even a new Heaven!

The Prophet Isaiah speaks of this plan of God:

"For behold, I create new heavens and a new earth; and the former
shall not be remembered or come to mind." (Isaiah 65:17)

The Psalms also reveal this prophetic Truth:

Of old You laid the foundation of the earth, and the
heavens are the work of Your hands. **They will perish**, *but*
You will endure; Yes, they will all grow old like a garment; like
a cloak You will change them, and they will be changed."
(Psalms 102:25, 26)

Even the Lord Jesus speaks into this as part of the plan of God. The exact work Jesus speaks here is an important one – it is the word *regeneration*.

"So Jesus said to them, "Assuredly I say to you, that in the
regeneration, *when the Son of Man sits on the throne of His*
Glory, you who have followed Me will also sit on twelve thrones,
judging the twelve tribes of Israel." (Matthew 19:28)

That word Jesus uses here is the Greek word *paliggenesia*. It literally means re-generation, hence renovation, regeneration, the production of a new life consecrated to God, a radical change of mind for the better. The word was often used to denote the restoration of a thing – to its original pristine state, by renovation, renewal or restoration of life after death. It means re-creation.

It is the ultimate plan of God! It is like unto restoring us back to a garden of Eden, like returning to a state of absolute purity, and unbroken fellowship with God. How awesome is that?

But when will this happen? Great question! Here is what the Word of God says about it:

> "...And that He may send Jesus Christ, who was preached to you before, whom heaven must receive <u>until</u> the times of **restoration** of all things, which God has spoken by the mouth of all His Holy Prophets since the world began." (Acts 3:20, 21)

The word *restoration* here is the word *apokatastasis*, and it means restoration back to a true Theocracy, of a perfect state – before the fall! Reconstitution, restitution.

> "Now I saw a **new heaven and a new earth**, for the first heaven and the first earth had passed away. Also there was no more sea.
>
> Then I, John, saw the holy city, New Jerusalem, coming down out of heaven from God, prepared as a bride adorned for her husband. And I heard a loud voice from heaven saying, "Behold, the tabernacle of God is with men, and He will dwell with them, and they shall be His people. God Himself will be with them and be their God. And God will wipe away every tear from their eyes; there shall be no more death, nor sorrow, nor crying. There shall be no more pain, for the former things have passed away."
>
> Then He who sat on the throne said, "**Behold, I make all things new.**" And He said to me, "Write, for these words are true and faithful." (Revelation 21:1-5)

What a glorious future we have in Christ Jesus! No more tears, no more sickness, no more curse! For all eternity, living in the radiant Presence of God and worshipping Him forever more!

"And there shall be no more curse, but the throne of God and of the Lamb shall be in it, and His servants shall serve Him." (Revelation 22:3)

How will the Lord perform this transformation? Like He has done almost everything else… with His Holy Fire!!!

*"But the heavens and the earth which are now preserved by the same word, **are reserved for fire** until the day of judgment and perdition of ungodly men.*

But, beloved, do not forget this one thing, that with the Lord one day is as a thousand years, and a thousand years as one day. The Lord is not slack concerning His promise, as some count slackness, but is longsuffering toward us, not willing that any should perish but that all should come to repentance.

The Day of the Lord

*But the day of the Lord will come as a thief in the night, in which the heavens will pass away with a great noise, and the elements will melt with fervent heat; **both the earth and the works that are in it will be burned up.** Therefore, since all these things will be dissolved, what manner of persons ought you to be in holy conduct and godliness, looking for and hastening the coming of the day of God, because of which the heavens will be dissolved, **being on fire**, and the elements will melt with fervent heat? Nevertheless we, according to His promise, look for new heavens and a new earth in which righteousness dwells." (2 Peter 3:7-13)*

In the end, Jesus will have done it all! He will complete the ultimate plan given to Him by His Father in creating a glorious

226

family! (We know Jesus created man because the Bible says nothing was created without Him), that we would one day become the Lamb King's wife and rule and reign with Him for all eternity is astounding!

But knowing that man would sin, Jesus agreed to leave Heaven to come to earth to redeem His creation through the atoning, agonizing death on a cross.

But before entering humanity Himself as the promised Messiah, Jesus first came in many visitations (Christophanies) throughout the Old Testament, leading His people forward towards God's Ultimate & Great Plan – almost always, in a manifestation of His Holy Fire!

Then the born King became man and entered His ministry and mission upon the earth at around age 30. John the Baptist said He would baptize with the Holy Spirit and Fire. Jesus Himself declared that He came to bring fire upon the earth (there is both a natural and spiritual connotation to that declaration).

Seven days after His ascension, that full purpose came forth – as the Holy Spirit came and baptized and birthed the Church of Jesus Christ in Holy Fire!

Jesus, the Wonderful Counselor, made it clear that His counsel was for us to buy gold *from* Him, gold tried in the fire! He was longing to have His Holy fire burn away all the dross and impurities from our lives in this lifetime. Why? Because He declared that one day, every man's work would be tested by His Holy Fire to prove and preserve that which is precious and of God (gold, silver, and precious jewels), and to burn up the rest (wood, hay, and stubble), which is worthless!

*"For no other foundation can anyone lay than that which is laid, which is Jesus Christ. Now if anyone builds on this foundation with **gold**, silver, precious stones, wood, hay, straw, each one's work will become clear; for the Day will declare it, because it will be revealed by fire; and the fire will test each one's work, of what sort it is. If anyone's work which he has built on it endures, he will receive a reward. If anyone's work is burned, he will suffer loss; but he himself will be saved, yet so as through fire."*
(1 Corinthians 3:11-15)

At some point in time Jesus, the King of Fire will return. There are many different views of what that will look like, but most agree there is a time of a Millennial Reign, where Christ Jesus will reign upon the earth for a thousand years.

But there is also an appointed time in this incredible plan of the ages, where Jesus takes everything He has accomplished from down through the entirety of time itself – to the very end where even the final foe is conquered – death. And then Jesus takes it all, in complete success and victory and gives the entire Kingdom back to the Father – fulfilling the eternal purposes of God the Father!

"For as in Adam all die, even so in Christ all shall be made alive. But each one in his own order: Christ the first–fruits, afterward those who are Christ's at His coming. Then comes the end, when He delivers the Kingdom to God the Father, when He puts an end to all rule and all authority and power. For He must reign till He has put all enemies under His feet. The last enemy that will be destroyed is death. For "He has put all things under His feet." But when He says "all things are put under Him," it is evident that He who put all things under Him is excepted. Now when all things are made subject to Him, then the Son Himself will also be subject to Him who put all things under Him, that God may be all in all." (1 Corinthians 15:22-28

Isn't that awesome! Then comes the time that our Mighty God will literally create a new Heaven and a new Earth! The old cursed earth and the former Heaven will all be dissolved, and then the most glorious thing will happen:

> *"And he showed me a pure river of water of life, clear as crystal, proceeding from the throne of God and of the Lamb. In the middle of its street, and on either side of the river, was the* **Tree of Life***, which bore twelve fruits, each tree yielding its fruit every month. The leaves of the Tree were for the healing of the nations. And there shall be* **no more curse***, but the Throne of God and of the Lamb shall be in it, and His servants shall serve Him. They shall see His face, and His name shall be on their foreheads. There shall be no night there: They need no lamp nor light of the sun, for the Lord God gives them Light. And they shall reign forever and ever." (Revelation 22:1-5)*

What a marvelous plan carried out in absolute perfection! From start to finish our God had our best interests at heart. Look at what He did! He restores us to the pre-fall condition as pure vessels with no sin or curse. He placed us back in a Garden of Eden type setting – with the Tree of Life right in the middle of it! And this time, there is no Tree of the Knowledge of Good & Evil in sight – because there is no more evil – it has been burned up in Holy Fire of God's final judgments, and we will dwell together with God and with our Lamb Lion King Jesus *forever*!

A NEW HEAVEN AND A NEW EARTH

Other Books By Timothy D. Johnson

ORDER BOOKS AT: www.btjohnsonpublishing.com

Timothy D. Johnson
P.O. Box 100
Battle Ground, WA 98604

timothyjohnson107@gmail.com